Apartness:

A Memoir in Essays and Poems

Judy Kronenfeld

AN INLANDIA INSTITUTE PUBLICATION

INLANDIA
INSTITUTE

RIVERSIDE, CALIFORNIA

Apartness: A Memoir in Essays and Poems by Judy Kronenfeld

ISBN: 978-1-955969-38-3
eISBN: 978-1-955969-39-0

Library of Congress Control Number: 2024047692
Copyright © 2025 Judy Kronenfeld

Permissions
Inlandia Institute
4178 Chestnut Street
Riverside CA 92501

Printed and bound in the United States
Distributed by Ingram

Cover art: Lavina Blossom
Book layout & design: Mark Givens
Publications Coordinator: Laura Villareal

Published by Inlandia Institute
Riverside, California
www.InlandiaInstitute.org
First Edition

Apartness:

A Memoir in Essays and Poems

Judy Kronenfeld

Also by Judy Kronenfeld

POETRY

Disappeared Down Dark Wells, and Still Falling
Ghost Nurseries
Shadow of Wings
Light Lowering in Diminished Sevenths
Shimmer
Bird Flying through the Banquet
Groaning and Singing
If Only There Were Stations of the Air
Oh Memory, You Unlocked Cabinet of Amazements!

CRITICISM

KING LEAR and the Naked Truth: Rethinking the Language of Religion and Resistance

These essays by Judy Kronenfeld tell their tales through the eyes of a passionate poet as well as from the heart of a devoted daughter and from the skilled mind of a consummate scholar. Many writers share the state of "apartness"—often standing outside "real life" as an intense observer, sometimes feeling disconnected and alone. Kronenfeld expresses these conflicting states while leaning toward the attractiveness of living a committed Jewish life and rejecting the limitations of becoming a devoted member of a religion. As a daughter she guides both her mother and father through the devastating ills of old age and as a mother she cherishes the trials and triumphs of her two grown children. The reader appreciates her insightful narratives, while being drawn into the emotional immediacy expressed in the individual poems that complement and illuminate each moving essay. A beautiful and complicated book.

    –Merrill Joan Gerber, author of *Revelation at the Food Bank* and *The Kingdom of Brooklyn*

Judy Kronenfeld's memoir weaves exposition and poetry to create a nuanced, poignant, and sometimes humorous portrait of life as an outsider in a predominantly Christian culture. Though her Eastern European Jewish background is often in the foreground, Kronenfeld addresses other kinds of "apartness" as well: the American abroad, the aged, the frail. In a country that sees itself as a melting pot but is increasingly tribal, Kronenfeld captures the feeling of being incorporated in neither. Spanning several decades, she illuminates past inequities and prejudices, though those are not the primary concerns of this work. Despite the beautiful specificity of the stories she tells, this is a book for everyone, written with intelligence, compassion, and an unflinching self-awareness.

    –Betsy Mars, author of *Alinea* and *In the Muddle of the Night* (with Alan Walowitz)

Apartness is an unusual and splendid memoir, both engaging and moving. Kronenfeld seamlessly integrates prose recollections and reflective poetry as she takes the reader on a highly personal journey of joy, surprise, and sadness. In the process she creates a contemplative exploration of self, a love letter to her family, and a continuous reconsideration of her ethnic and religious heritage. Over and over I found myself stopping, chuckling, and nodding my head when encountering Kronenfeld's revealing flashes of insight drawn from the many challenging and intimate moments of her life. This is a book to be read with pleasure, as well as one to be recalled with joy.

–**Carlos E. Cortés**, author of *Rose Hill: An Intermarriage before Its Time* and *The Making—and Remaking —of a Multiculturalist*

What a gorgeous exploration of otherness, one that ultimately reminds us how deeply we're connected through the vulnerabilities of the body, the ache and bewilderment of loss. *Apartness* is seamless in its weave of poetry and essay, the membrane between the genres porous. Judy Kronenfeld's poetry shines through her prose, dappling her sentences with metaphor; she describes her Jewishness as "highly diluted, weak as a fifth cup of tea brewed with the same teabag," the ingratiation of her immigrant mother as "something like a savings account into which one put money against the nasty turns of cold fate."

"Maybe it is language itself that I am worshipping," Kronenfeld muses, and that devotion courses through each of these pages. Language is where this "unbelonging unbelonger" seems to find a true sense of home. She creates a welcome home on the page for readers, as well, a place where we can all be apart together, where we can remember we are part of it all. "You still see nothing / that is not there," she writes, "but now you sense everything / that is."

–**Gayle Brandeis**, author of *Drawing Breath: Essays on Writing, the Body, and Loss* and *The Book of Dead Birds*

Acknowledgments

The following essays, prose poems or flash memoir pieces, and the following poems originally appeared—sometimes in earlier versions or under somewhat different titles—in the publications listed below:

PROSE

Bear Flag Republic: Prose Poems and Poetics from California, ed. Christopher Buckley and Gary Young: "Resident Dead"
Hippocampus Magazine: "Shame"
Inlandia: A Literary Journey: "Blue Bowl of Sky"
Kaleidoscope: Exploring the Experience of Disability through Literature & the Fine Arts: "Operating in French"
The Press-Enterprise (Inlandia Literary Journeys Column): "The Two Coasts of the Mind"
Under the Sun:
  "Brief Dip into Ethnicity"
  "Death and Belief: the View from Without"
  "From Bagels, via George Herbert's *Temple,* to OMG! the Temple"
  "From Klein's to Saks with Mom: Remembrance of Shopping Past"
  "Half-Deaf, Half-Adjusted"
  "Looking Back: Why I Stopped Writing Poetry and How I Started Again: Embracing the Authentic, Contingent Self"
  "Medical Management of High-Maintenance Mom"
  "Speaking French"
Voices of Alzheimer's (The Healing Project): "Woosh"

POETRY

Avatar Review: "Chronic This and That"

Barnwood: "Miracles of the Kingdom of Sleep"

Cimarron Review: "In the Doctor's Office, Two Weeks before His Death"

Cyclamens and Swords: "Noblesse Oblige"

Innisfree Poetry Journal: "Minding Desert Places—Winter 4 P.M."

Montserrat Review: "Waiting for News Which Could Be Really Bad"

Poemeleon: "Ex-New Yorker Remembers Her Natural Landscape"

Poetica: "Revisiting the Metaphysicals: Two Scenes"

Poetry International: "Yiddish Kisses"

Poetry Midwest: "Useless Knowledge"

Snake Nation: "Decorum: An Immigrant Elegy"

Tipton Poetry Journal: "4 A.M., Suddenly Awake"

Verse Virtual: "Charm," "A Familiar Train of Religious Observances"

Wilshire Review: "Agnostic Psalm"

Author's Notes

The writing and publication of these essays and poems spans a period of at least 28 years, from about 1994 to 2022. The essays and other prose in this collection were thus written from the standpoint of particular moments in time—often much closer to the experience described than to the present; they vary in tonality and approach. A poem chosen from my books of poetry follows each essay, heightening or complicating the experiences involved. There has been no attempt to update or change the rootedness of the essays (or the poems) in the times in which they were written or their particular perspectives on the past.

Except for the names of my immediate family, living and dead (parents, spouse, children), I have not used the actual names of any persons, living or dead. Instead, I use initials (e.g. Dr. N., Mr. A.); these are not the actual initials of these persons. There is one exception; I do cite the actual name of a high school teacher in an endnote, because I reference an oral history project she was part of.

TABLE OF CONTENTS

Why I Stopped Writing And How I Started Again: Embracing the
Authentic, Contingent Self...13
Revisiting the Metaphysicals: Two Scenes 29

From Klein's to Saks with Mom: Remembrance of Shopping Past...........30
Decorum: An Immigrant Elegy...39

The Pregnant Body 42
Noblesse Oblige 50

Medical Management of High Maintenance Mom 51
Waiting for News Which Could Be Really Bad 75

Death and Belief: The View from Without 77
Agnostic Psalm 91

Speaking French 92
Charm 103

Resident Dead..106
Useless Knowledge 108

Woosh!...110
Yiddish Kisses 118

Shame..120
In the Doctor's Office, Two Weeks before His Death 122

Brief Dip into Ethnicity 124
Miracles of the Kingdom of Sleep.....................................135

Half-Deaf, Half-Adjusted...138
Chronic This and That..147

The Two Coasts of the Mind 148
Minding Desert Places—Winter, 4 P.M. 151

Blue Bowl of Sky...152
Ex-New Yorker Remembers Her Natural Landscape........................156

From Bagels, via George Herbert's *Temple*, to OMG! the Temple 158
A Familiar Train of Religious Observances............................174

Operating in French...176
4 A.M., Suddenly Awake...191

Why I Stopped Writing And How I Started Again: Embracing the Authentic, Contingent Self

As many writers are fond of saying, we don't choose our subjects; they choose us. In my case, my subjects tapped me on the shoulder or whispered in my ear, but, for a long time, I didn't hear or stifled them. And that has to do with cultural, historical and psychological factors that my analytical self has begun to understand. I *stopped* writing before I fully started—and that implies something about what it takes to write (and what it took to resume). My story is about the interaction of a person with family, culture, institutions, time and place—material for a complex novel—and so, necessarily somewhat schematized here. It is hardly unique, probably similar to many writers' or artists' stories, if not in the letter, in the spirit.

Many people have written about their own experience within a particular cultural context. This has become more common since the ascendance of memoir about relatively ordinary people as well as exceptional ones. But in my long-gone formative years and in the culture of my birth, repression was the better part of valor. It has taken me quite a while to claim my perspective.

I am first-generation American, the only child of Jewish immigrant parents. My father, born in Germany, came to this country in 1934, the year after Hitler came to power. Although most of my father's family escaped the Holocaust, his eldest sister and her husband and children were later murdered in Auschwitz. My mother was from Galicia in the Austro-Hungarian Empire. Probably born in the small town, Halich, she moved with her family to the city of Lemberg, now L'viv, about 70 miles away (both places now in the Ukraine), and later to Vienna; she emigrated to the U.S. from there in 1927. She didn't tell me about Lemberg until she was 65; she never mentioned

Halich, either, although it is listed as her place of birth, as well as the birthplace of her mother and most of her siblings on the ship manifest of the Olympic on which they sailed to New York, following their father who had emigrated some years before.

I grew up in a three-room apartment in a lower-middle-class immigrant neighborhood in the Bronx—Jews from Eastern Europe and Russia, Italians, and Irish. The apartment consisted of a kitchen, a living room (where my parents slept on a hide-a-bed sofa) and a bedroom (which they generously gave to me), as well as a bathroom, of course. Thus, I spent much of my childhood longing for a four-room apartment which would have a bedroom for my parents as well as one for me. A four-room apartment wouldn't always be in transition, would feel infinitely more formal, and wouldn't embarrass me when the few friends I had the courage to invite came over and asked where my parents slept.

Our building was next door to an Orthodox synagogue, which we attended only one time that I can recall during my childhood. Though my mother did observe the domestic Jewish rituals connected with food—she kept kosher and cooked special Sabbath, High Holiday, and Passover meals—my parents couldn't afford the synagogue dues (we were close to the poorest in my mother's and father's families), and they didn't have much time—apart from work and household maintenance—for synagogue attendance. My father worked a long day as a pattern-cutter in my mother's oldest brother's doll factory, and later, as a foreman in another factory. After that, he and my mother both got up in the wee hours of the morning six days a week in order to be ready for the 7:00 a.m. opening of the small luncheonette/candy store they bought in lower Manhattan. They were finally petit-bourgeois shopkeepers, but still so very working-class in style of life.

Throughout my childhood, I heard the Hebrew melodies morning and night and High Holy Days wafting from next door, and I imbibed a kind of vapor of religion, if not the genuine draft, along with a fairly intense sense of ethnic and class identity.

The author's parents at their lower Manhattan luncheonette. Early 1960s.

~

My parents produced a child with the immigrant values of hard work and perseverance, a desire to please and be accepted, to fit in, get ahead, and make good. The emphasis on "making a good impression" was huge, involving that mysterious essence, in the Bronxese of my 50s youth—*poysonality*. My parents modeled using it to ingratiate themselves with others. And indeed, immigrants who want to be accepted probably wisely figure out that they can't afford to represent themselves as anything less than ideally adjusted, as well as thrilled with *you*, the established American, who deigns to listen to their hearts and lungs with a stethoscope or to buy the merchandise they are selling. In the already conformist 50s, my parents—strong believers in the efficacy of that rosy self-presentation for winning friends and influencing people—did not exactly encourage nonconformist individualism and radical self-expression.

Nevertheless, I did write prose and poetry as a naïve child and as an adolescent, gifted by a doting uncle with many books, encouraged by my mother's pride in the skills of her American offspring, and by lessons in "creative writing" in elementary and junior high school, which tended to endorse the two happy adjectives before each noun school of aesthetics ("fluffy white clouds," "delicate pink petals"). But one of the pressures *against* writing that I felt from early on in my nuclear family was my mother's clear desire that all representations of our household and family be outstandingly cheerful and *rosy*. Perhaps that sunny ideal was even shared by the educational system in my immigrant world. In seventh grade, a teacher summarily wrote on a slightly melancholy essay of mine: "You are too young for *weltshmerz*"—that is, world weariness, romantic discontent.

"Writing," says the novelist Merrill Joan Gerber, "was the only place one could be totally honest; in all other areas of life the opposite was required. This put a great strain on me; it was an acrobatic feat always to have to say the correct (untrue) thing."[1] My own social and psychological circumstances and my youth itself didn't allow me to be that confident about honest self-expression.

~

I commuted to an entrance exam public high school for "gifted girls" in glamorous Manhattan, a borough full of intimidatingly rich people, powerful people, men and women wearing suits—the women sporting little circle pins on their lapels. *Those* women probably wore negligees or silk lounging robes—just like in the movies—when they weren't in their suits. My mother wore a ratty "house dress"—an often partially torn, loose floral print—and shabby, frayed slippers when she wasn't dressed "for the street" in her "street dress"—and that was most of the time. Still, high school was a step up and away. I wrote well-turned sonnets about disappointed adolescent love for my adored and brilliant eleventh grade English teacher who didn't censor such melancholy, world-weary subjects. Thus encouraged, I contributed frequently to my high school literary magazine. And I tried mightily to identify with Manhattan. But this wasn't that easy since not only was the Bronx, where I returned each afternoon, painfully without glamour, but everyone from the Bronx spoke in a way that marked them as Bronxites; they spoke Bronxese, a *nasty* nasalized dialect that my high school considered a serious social liability. We had to attend classes to retrain our speech habits, to eradicate those terrible accents that would keep us stuck in the lower social classes for the rest of our blighted lives. Class embarrassment and ethnic minority embarrassment felt closely related to an upwardly mobile girl in the waspish 50s and early 60s.

~

Over three decades after that high school speech class I published a poem, "Relapsing into a Bronx Accent While Sitting on the Couch with My Daughter," which recalls how

> our obedient tongues
> pirouetted, en pointe, so
> to speak, unlearning steamy rooms,
> cabbage, brisket, men in underwear
> at the kitchen table, playing pinochle.

This poem actually embraces my lower-middle class Bronx first-generation roots—at least as a metaphor for a sort of relaxed earthiness. If in Manhattan they ate artichokes and (unkosher) lobster (foods I didn't get to sample until late in my teens), in the Bronx, that doting uncle got all excited when my mother made a dish out of calves' feet—a sort of Jewish soul food with an odd-sounding name, which I pretend to like for the sake of this poem:

Yet how good to unpack
and speak
the mother tongue—
even years later—

as good as releasing
numbed taped toes
from ballet shoes,

how good to tickle my wrinkling nose
with a feast
of truck-stop d's and t's
and *flayut* vowels,

Jeez! as good as
garlic-rubbed toast
and jellied calves' feet
that had a name
that sounded like a sneeze (*pcha!*),

as good as Ah!
rubbing your dirty feet,
my little big one.[2]

But it took me a long while to get to such a place. And my
college experience, if anything, fattened my little inner demons.

~

I went on scholarship to Smith, one of The Seven Sister col-
leges, an all-women's school definitely considered "elite" at the
time. At least fourth-fifths of the students seemed to be the
daughters and granddaughters of those rich and powerful Man-
hattan eaters of artichokes and lobster and wearers of silk
lounging robes. My sparsely-educated parents wanted their
child's life and social position to be better than theirs, and saw

education as the means, as I surely did myself. In addition, that marvelous high school English teacher had gone to Smith—one of five Black students at the time she attended, in the 40s[3]—and strongly urged me to apply. The fact that she wasn't an average Smithie encouraged me.

But first there was the process of getting in, with the hefty scholarship that would make it possible, a process that made me feel I was in training to become an imposter. I had to be interviewed, *at home*, in the living room slash parental bedroom of our three-room apartment, by the impeccably suited, circle-pinned Park Avenue Ladies of the Smith College Club of New York, who controlled recommendations about scholarships, and the interview had to be in the presence of my mother. As I knew she would, my mother followed her own inner cultural directives, serving bowl after bowl of fruit, plate after plate of cake and cookies, as if the ladies' disinclination to sample the goodies meant she hadn't yet hit on the right offering. Finally, when there was no room left on the coffee table, each of the ladies removed her gloves and politely accepted one very small cookie. My mother had the wisdom not to speak too much. But when she did speak, in her heavy German-Yiddish-New York accent, it was in what she fancied a genteel manner, as she extolled my fervent desire for the heavenly blessing of admission to Smith. I bit down my embarrassment and smiled and smiled and said humbly how honored I would be if they graced me with their largesse. I had to snuff out a tiny flame of pride (tiny, because I barely knew it could burn) about the bootlicking position I was taking which they seemed to respond to *quite* favorably. *Noblesse oblige.* Ingratiation—it *worked*.

And then came Smith itself. Even though I had managed to get there, and surely thought my being there was intellectually deserved, it was easy to feel like an *arriviste*. There were medieval Freudian customs like Father/Daughter Weekends. My dad drove the four or five hours during his backbreaking work week, laid his head on the desk in my Abnormal Psych class, and promptly fell asleep, causing my cheeks to flame, however much I loved him. I was acutely aware that my parents were very far from the professionals most of my peers' parents were, and vastly removed in finances and cultural style. The furnishings of the living and dining rooms in the "house" in which I lived were far nicer than what we had at home. There were linen napkins, and napkin rings, for heaven's sake, something I'd never seen. Girls wore jodhpurs—something else I'd never seen—rode horses, *owned* horses boarded nearby. There were silver tea and coffee services in the residences (the motif of the time was "gracious living"). I was so tongue-tied by class-consciousness that I was even afraid to approach the liveried doorman in the elegant Manhattan building where a wealthy friend from my Smith dorm lived. I would hang back from asking him to announce my presence when I arrived at the building to meet my friend for the drive back to Smith in her car.

I was also conscious of being from a minority culture as a person of Jewish background, not so much because there were no other Jewish women at Smith (there were a good number, and we all seemed to have been given Jewish roommates!), or because I experienced any overt anti-Semitism, but because, before the advent of multiculturalism, the dominant Protestant culture was so clearly the only game in town. Nondenominational chapel was Protestant nondenominational chapel. The very coolness of Ivy League or preppy culture—its esteem for the blasé attitude (more easily adopted by those quite content with their own socio-economic status)—seemed an implicit or even explicit raised eyebrow at ethnic excitability. Indeed, when I became enthusiastic in my 17th Century Poetry class—I did tend to get excited about literature—my professor encouraged me to moderate my tone and voice. In my graduation picture of black-robed women from my Smith house, a row standing on one leg behind those sitting, most everyone smiling and a few cracking up, I seem to be one of the most—if not the most—abandoned (second row, fourth from the right).

The author with other graduating seniors from her Smith dorm. 1964.

My body is tilted, my head thrown back and mouth wide open in unselfconscious glee, my knee definitely not lifted genteelly, like one of the other women's in the back row, showing off a shapely calf; instead my leg is plopped without forethought, flat on the shoulders of the two women sitting in front of me, so that my full broad kneecap is exposed and my calf appears thicker than the calves stretching into the front row on my right and left. Oh, enthusiasm was definitively not genteel. It was lower-class and too ethnic.

~

Even the reigning approach to literature when I was an undergraduate, the "New Criticism," valued cold perfections, encouraging poetry of restraint, impersonality, and ironic distance. It tended to devalue the personal, to exclude social, cultural, political and historical contexts. Yale's Department of English, housing such luminaries as Robert Penn Warren, Cleanth Brooks and W. K. Wimsatt, was "the foremost center"[4] of the "New Criticism" in the 50s and 60s, and the seedbed of its dissemination to nearby places like Smith, some of whose faculty had obtained their advanced degrees there. The atmosphere in the English Department at Yale in the early 50s, when its soon-to-be illustrious (and sui generis) professor Harold Bloom was in grad school, has been described as "very High Church and stiff." And Bloom himself (born of Yiddish-speaking immigrant parents, and raised in the Bronx, like myself) has been described as a grad student who was already "big and messy and emotional … in a department whose Anglophilia often functioned as a genteel form of anti-Semitism…."[5] Indeed, "in the traditionally Anglophilic circle of academic English … Yale's social reputation [was] one of wealth and class."[6] The early 60s, when I was at Smith, were much like the 50s; revolutionary cultural and social changes did not begin until after I graduated.

The clincher to my experience of—well, I have to call it a sort of inauthenticity—was probably my exposure to that reigning school of literary criticism. Now, the New Critical approach had enormous virtues of close attention to texts and their formal features, virtues that definitely contributed to my scholarly, and, ultimately, even to my creative development. I loved even the "controlled" poetry I was reading as an undergraduate, perhaps because its control, like the control of baroque music, suggested emotions all the stormier for requiring restraint. But the manner in which poetry was presented in class had the effect of making the young potential writer think writing was solely canonical and not something a living contemporary could do—especially a woman, and a minority woman at that. That manner of teaching made it hard to think that poems—no matter how refined and revised—came out of feeling, that they were expressions of lived experience and the need to explore and capture it, rather than elegant collections of poetic devices that were simply willed into being out of a disinterested desire to create a perfect artifact.

At my first college seminar at a faculty home—on the English novel—I ventured to ask a question about the eighteenth-century economic and social context of Daniel Defoe's *Moll Flanders*—and was stonily stared into silence. What did all this avoidance of social and economic contexts mean? Were writers imposters, suppressing ungenteel backgrounds like my own? Or worse, were they true aristocrats born to the purple, and didn't need to mention their socially pure origins?

Looking back on these experiences, I think of a moment from Woody Allen's 1977 movie *Annie Hall*. "Alvy" imagines how he appears to Annie's family when he's at their prim lace-covered table—as if he were wearing a rabbinical beard and side curls. Watching that movie, even as a long-married parent in the 80s, I still blushingly felt Alvy's shame and identified with the lower-class Jewish culture he mentally contrasts with Annie's family's decorum: in an apartment rattled by the El, food is eaten almost standing up, with a haunch on the table; a female relative grabs his cheek between thumb and bent forefinger and shakes it in greeting.

I suppose every bildungsroman is a story of feeling left out of *something*. Members of sturdy but perhaps vanilla majorities may feel left out of the color, warmth, and bondedness of ethnic or religious minorities. Children of hippie parents may long for apple pie American lifestyles. I longed for the effortless sense of ease—a sort of sprezzatura—and of belonging and privilege enjoyed by what Philip Roth's Nathan Zuckerman calls "the monied Protestant hierarchy that had reigned over Boston and

New York society while [his] own poor ancestors were being ruled by rabbis in the ghettos of Eastern Europe,"[7] although I might not have been able to state my longing in such terms at the time.

All of these circumstances, then, led to a frame of mind inimical to exploring my emotions and experiences in poetry or any other creative expression (although I did write an intensely text-based honors thesis, also critical of the ahistorical tendencies of the New Criticism, that earned me a B.A. *summa cum laude!*). This frame of mind persisted for me for almost twenty years after I graduated from college, until the early 80s when, in my forties, I rededicated myself to writing poetry. It's not as if I didn't thrive intellectually in college and graduate school; I surely did. But the creative writer in me was not nourished or developed very much at all. I kept a sporadic journal which I showed no one. I took one undergrad creative writing course in fiction and poetry in which I performed modestly. I wrote poems here and there on my own, some of which I submitted to the college literary magazine, which roundly rejected them. I found the editors snooty, and gave up. I lacked discipline, the wherewithal for revision, regular feedback from others—whether amateur or professional, consistent exposure to contemporary work. When leaving (for family reasons) a tenure-track job teaching English at a Midwestern university in the 70s, and thinking vaguely again of "returning" to poetry, I was quite vulnerable to a comment from a colleague: "Why do you want to get involved in all that emotional stuff?"

~

Poetry can't begin, says the poet Jane Hirshfield, if you have not conquered your "fear of public exposure, of being found unacceptable if [you] speak honestly, if who [you] really are were to become known,"[8] however complex and paradoxical that "you" is,

I might add. I believe the statement holds true for other creative work as well, such as personal essays—like those in this book— and even short stories, though it's more possible to disguise the self in fiction.

There are many reasons I was gradually able to conquer that fear of self-exposure enough to write, revise, submit and publish poetry, the more occasional short story, as well as, from my fifties on, personal essays. One major enabler was certainly the sheer process of growing up, the passage of time taking me from being a child in my natal family, vulnerable to parental and cultural pressures, to an adult parent in my own family with its own status and culture (in an America where there can be class mobility, thankfully, even startling mobility, through education). Changes in the cultural atmosphere with feminism and a variety of movements broadening that "Anglophile" emphasis in literary studies and creative work, and even the rise of highly personal truth-telling in memoir are other cultural elements that have worked to my advantage as a writer. I was fortunate, too, to be able to participate in an informal public poetry workshop led by a kind and brilliant teacher with no formal credentials (she did not write or publish poetry) at the California university where I had taught composition and literature, and, eventually, to participate in a poetry group I started with a local writer. Thus I began a lifetime of sharing my work in a congenial setting, getting feedback, revising according to my own understandings, as well as learning, first-hand, that writing, however necessarily well crafted, is often sparked by the very vulnerabilities and fears of self-exposure I had thought might keep me from it. I was also fortunate in being able to teach creative writing at that same California university soon after my rededication to the craft, further schooling myself in contemporary poetry, fiction, and creative nonfiction, and in practical criticism, building on the habits of close reading I had gained from my New Critical undergraduate years. I learned—both consciously and unconsciously—from the authors I read and used as models, as well as from the students' work I commented on and hoped to bring to greater proficiency.

But, given my first-generation American and rather Puritan nose-to-the-grindstone leanings and the concepts I internalized from my own academic experience, one part of me originally did think much too academically about poetry, that is, that poems just might be elegant collections of poetic devices that *could* simply be willed into being out of a disinterested desire to create a perfect artifact. I had to learn otherwise. As the poet William Stafford says:

> Poetry is the kind of thing you have to see from the corner of your eye. You can be too well prepared for poetry. A conscientious interest in it is worse than no interest at all. It's like a very faint star. If you look right at it you can't see it, but if you look a little to one side it is there.[9]

Even if there are certain melodies that repeatedly play within us, poems do come from our contingent selves, the selves we are at particular transient moments in time, selves that are going to feel slightly different in an hour, and maybe quite different tomorrow. There are no maps. Every poet has some methods to tap into that contingent self, to reach the universal *through* the particular and transient, to sneak up on the authentic and effective. Poems have to be snuck up on because they can come from places in the psyche that are full of tension and contradiction. (And also because a slantwise rather than head on approach is usually intrinsic to their effect.) I often need the "permission" that certain poems I stumble on or reread may give me—there's definitely an element of accident in all this—to write about something equally true or disturbing or secret or daring, or surprisingly joyful, or comic or trivial—or all of these.

One of my methods is to gradually accumulate scraps of paper with thoughts, images, ideas, and lines in a file folder, and to type these up every once in a while (which can result in some unexpected juxtapositions as unrelated ideas fall against each other and sometimes spark). Later, I return to the collections of typed up scraps to get started again. Because we are constantly changing, yet also do have those melodies that keep playing within us, certain of the images or sensations we recorded will appeal to us at the very moment we are getting ready to write and lead to a line, a stanza, or the rough draft of an entire poem. Others will seem dull or uninteresting. But all it takes is the one or two that compel at a particular moment in time.

Until well into my forties, it was difficult for me to mention or write about any subject or experience it would have been a *shanda*—Yiddish for a shame, scandal or disgrace—to reveal. Even worse would have been a *shanda fur die goyim*—literally a "shame in front of the nations"—which occurs when a Jew reveals something (or behaves in a way) that confirms non-Jews' stereotypes about Jews. For me, such subjects, or indeed, revelations, included my parents' very modest means—emblematized by that hide-a-bed sofa in the living room that they slept on—their limited education that I once found embarrassing, and their harsh words to one another, in spite of their need for each other. Also included were such locales as the live kosher poultry store in the primeval peasant Bronx of my childhood where chickens were slaughtered on the spot, their blood draining into the straw-covered floor, their feathers smoked off with a lit candle, causing a putrid stink. Included as well were remembered gestures—like my mom's superstitious fake-spitting twice, while saying *poo-poo* (apparently the gesture and the sound both required) to ward off the evil eye when something praiseworthy was said about her only child—a gesture that would have utterly mortified me in front of my Smith friends, for sure. Yet these moments and matters stuck with me, and sometimes were the memory seeds that began to grow poems, or contributed to the verisimilar detail that propelled my poems forward. The Yiddish that sometimes embarrassed me as a child began to warm some of those poems, too.

Once the gates opened, and stayed open for such inclusions in my poems, vulnerabilities personally experienced and observed, contradictions and tensions in pivotal memories still faintly stinging began to be explorable in the more discursive form of the personal essay. Dense knots of psychological pain, humiliation, and injustice, or of sorrow, frustration, and love could be unwound in this form. And once it became possible for me to share the multi-layered, contradictory truths of my life, it also became possible to share other remembrances—of pleasure and joy, beauty, and even belonging.

I suppose I hardly need to say *Go figure!*

Revisiting the Metaphysicals: Two Scenes

At the round earth's imagin'd corners, blow
Your trumpets, Angells, and arise, arise
From death, you numberlesse infinities
Of soules...
   –John Donne

In my dream I hear
one long shofar blast and my family
gathers—weakly kicking out of graves,
reassembling from the gritty dust
of outlawed urns—summoned
by my wildly cooking resurrected mother.
They sit haunch
to haunch in the chapel of her
kitchen: *All whom ... age, agues... despair ...*
hath slain, drinking her healing
broth, chewing her meats stewed
in their own juices, soup-to-nuts
revivified, transformed,

as I was in the chapel of Smith College—
in my plaid kilt with its fake
gold pin, my knee socks, my penny
loafers—sending forth
on my own young voice with the other
girls' lifted voices, the lofty strains
of Protestant America, translated at last
from the crumbly Bronx
of brisket, kosher chickens, soup
greens, on the brink
of the Glory of my life.

From Klein's to Saks with Mom: Remembrance of Shopping Past

My mother was always a serious student of ads. They were religiously regarded sources of information about the new country—the goyim, the insiders—for immigrant Jews and their first-generation children; they were also escapes into a land where beneficently smiling husbands allowed their delightedly smiling wives to hook arms with them, as they both glanced back—on their way out the door for some clearly joint pleasure trip—at the new automatic washer churning automatically away. My mother read the fashion ads the way William Carlos Williams implied people should read poems, and she always got the news there, whether she could implement it for herself or not. Though she often spent whole days in her "house dress," and preserved unpublic items of clothing such as pajamas and robes until they quite literally hung by a thread, and though she usually didn't even glance at any items for herself when she shopped with me, she loved to dress well when she dressed up, and she loved to see me dressed well; she was known in our small extended family for her "eye," for having good taste.

The author's mother in her "street" clothes. 1940s?

APARTNESS

On shopping Saturdays in the 50s, like those aimed at new clothes for school, Mother and I would take the subway from the Bronx early in the morning. Our destination was posh midtown Manhattan, Fifth Avenue, a cultural divide away. When I was in high school and our economic circumstances had improved somewhat (my father making a slightly better salary as foreman at a new toy factory than as a fabric-cutter on the floor of his brother-in-law's doll factory), we aimed first for Lord and Taylor's at 38th and Fifth (I can still picture the insouciance of their logo script!), rather than Alexander's in the Bronx, or the S. Klein's of my elementary school days, at Union Square and 14th Street, or even Ohrbach's on 34th Street, which had some very small pretensions to luxe.

When I was a young child, I didn't even have expectations that made S. Klein depressing, though—especially since late middle age—I've found "bargain basements" more and more dispiriting, because of the stamina and patience and coping with sensory overload required to shop in them, as well as their sad smell of pinched circumstances. The most dispiriting such store I have ever encountered was in Montmartre: sloping wooden floors, tables piled high with merchandise looking no different from rags, people stampeding through like cattle just released from shunts, frenzied arms elbowing other frenzied arms as hands claw through the goods. But, oh, Lord and Taylor's was genteel. No sweaters dropped from hangers to catch beneath your heels, no cocktail dresses dragged in the dust beneath the racks, their luster dimmed. No broken zippers, missing buttons, belts switched by previous tryers-on, no size 16s mixed with the 10s to dampen the shopper's spirit. There were discreetly attentive saleswomen on the floor, attractively made-up, wearing heels and smart "street dresses," that item of clothing in strong disjunctive contrast to those ubiquitous loose "house dresses" my mother donned on ordinary days when she did not have to travel downtown for her own job on the floor of her brother's factory, but stayed at home to tackle the endless task of cleaning our small apartment.

There was in the New York of my 40s and 50s childhood a tremendous divide between "the street" and "the house" as far as decorum went. In the house, and even sometimes—if with reluctance and some shame—when my mother, carrying bags of garbage, took the elevator to the basement incinerator, she wore cold cream on her face, those torn and patched house dresses, those slippers almost in shreds. For the street, most assuredly for downtown, she put on her "two-way stretch" girdle, stockings and heels, and a skirt and blouse or dress, often accompanied by a costume jewelry necklace; she powdered her face, penciled in (increasingly sloppily) her barely-there-brows, made a bow of her mouth and applied bright red lipstick (inevitably to her two front teeth as well), and sometimes even added the obligatory swathe of pearlescent blue eye shadow on each lid that signaled being "dressed" in the 50s.

The saleswomen at Lord and Taylor's sometimes spoke in somewhat cultivated accents, as if the tones of their clientele had rubbed off on them, or their sheer interest in being of service had slowed down and smoothed out the Bronx and Brooklyn brogues that were their birthrights. But the slightly cultivated air they coveted could not be mistaken for the manners of matrons to the manor born, like the three Park Avenue ladies in circle pins and pearls who later interviewed me in our tiny apartment for the scholarship to that Ivy League women's college (we called it a "girl's school" then) I won in 1960. Still, those circle pins and the tasteful suits that went with them were for sale, and what probably most qualified those Bronx and Brooklyn saleswomen for their Lord and Taylor jobs was their eager desire to purchase those items for their own daughters (an eagerness, like my mother's—and mine—disparaged in the understated-to-a-fault Ivy League). Their manner, then, in bringing in to the dressing room that A-line in the hunter green which would be "just poifect" for me, or the classic black sheath in a size 10 which wouldn't crease around my hips was what my mother—with her eye for quality and line and her contempt for ostentation and useless expenditure—might have called *haimish*: domestic, homelike, unpretentious. It was a word my mother used in the only linguistic play I ever recall her engaging in; when our small family visited Amish country in Pennsylvania, she announced gleeful at her own wit, oblivious to her mispronunciation: "The *Amish* are *haimish*."

~

When we got off the subway at 42nd and Sixth Avenue, my mother was vibrant, energized by the streaming hordes; she strode forcefully past the library lions, eyes wide, as if we were rushing for the freshest produce, just in from the farms, before it was picked over. Indeed, she seemed to relish shopping for produce, too, on her marketing days in the Bronx, especially if I came along; haimishly she'd coddle pears with "red cheeks," as if picturing how delicious they'd look ripening further in the wicker basket on the kitchen table, how nutritiously their juices would infiltrate the blood of her first-and-only born.

Indefatigable, she would shlep me from Lord and Taylor, if that didn't yield the find, to Saks or Peck and Peck, or even down to Ohrbach's. The only permitted break was lunch at the crowded counter of Chock Full o' Nuts: a nutted cream cheese sandwich on raisin bread, and, of course, her fuel, coffee.

Decades later—after my parents had moved to my Southern California town—although my mother's toes were infected because of diabetes and poor circulation, and it was just days before her vascular surgery, that engine was still running, that light in her eye could still be turned on, and I am ashamed to admit, I allowed our trip to purchase a robe for her hospital stay to take a detour when she said "we'll just take a look—for you." Just a few days before she died, my mother, two-strokes humbled, wet-thumbed through the glossy pages of a department store ad and said, "It's the Fourth of July—lots of sales—we should go."

Back in the 50s, my mother often shared with me that moment in the dressing room when the dress or outfit flirts with you, saying it could just possibly become yours, and you have to decide whether to go with it or send it the way of all the others. It was a moment always oddly better at home when you tried it on again, now that it *was* yours, flattering you more somehow than you thought it had in the store. Those dressing room moments usually came late in a long day of gauging what was in style, what was affordable, what was worth the higher price, and sometimes of going back for the first dress that winked at us. My mother smoothed some dresses over my butt with a frown, or asked me to stand sideways to see whether my stomach poufed out, and even sometimes invited the saleswoman in to corroborate her suspicions, causing my appalled embarrassment at her maternal ownership of my teenage body. She responded to my serious flirtations with a dress she herself liked by making the moment into a triumph, a victory over untold negative forces. She'd say things like, "I don't care what anybody says, you've *got* to have it!" It was then that she would think of my father, fending for himself alone at home on a Saturday, and, somewhat guiltily, find a pay phone to call him. She would be apologetic but excited, still full of store endorphins and sorry for the lateness of the hour, assuring him that the prize was worth it and that he would think so too. She'd sweet-talk him into meeting us at the deli or the cafeteria for dinner, since by the time we got home it would be "too late to cook." Virtuously tired, armed with shopping bags rustling with tissue paper, we took our deserved rest on the subway home.

After dinner, modeling was always required. Even in his old age, after my parents' move to California, my well-trained father expressed genuine delight on those rare occasions when I showed off a particularly important find. "That really shows off your figure," he said when I was 16 and when I was 46, as my figure underwent desired and undesired transformations, "it's really something." He'd mimic a wolf whistle and end with the benediction: "Wear it in good health." When I was young, the clothes for a new year of junior high or high school were sometimes taken along on the next day's Sunday outing for an imprimatur from the uncle who lived on the Island. My mother's youngest brother, the sometime-artist, the only one with a year of American college, would thoughtfully chew on his pipe and pronounce the verdict, validating everyone's taste.

Sometimes I wonder about the afterlife of clothes. Is the arty grey, red and black bias plaid A-line wool skirt with matching bateau neck top with three-quarter raglan sleeves that everyone liked as much as I did, and that I wore for years after the ninth grade with comfort and pleasure, now being worn by somebody somewhere in the U.S.? Or has it been exported to the third world? Or is it part of a rag rug, or just a rag, or is it dust?

~

I still miss those celebrative familial moments of material joy. These days my husband barely lifts his eyes from his crossword puzzle when I swish in, glittering, in some concoction for a family event, and his judgment almost never exceeds "It's fine." He has a saint-like patience when we shop together for me, but his enthusiasms are restricted to avatars of the old Radio Shack and the tool section of Home Depot. In more recent years, even when I am desperately trying to, I find I often cannot get these seemingly material pleasures back. When I have a few moments in a full week, I go alone to the local designer discount emporium, load up my cart with probable impossibles, and leave them all there at the door of the dressing room without trying them on. Sometimes, even then, I come out of the store feeling oddly rested. Worse are the days when I enter such a store, or even a nicer department store, am overwhelmed, wander the aisles aimlessly, picking up, fingering, then letting material slip through my fingers, until I leave in disgust. I think, then, of a couple of newfound shopping companions I overheard in the dressing room next to mine one day of desultory and solitary trying on of clothes that utterly failed to please. I had glimpsed the two out of the corner of my eye at the 60% off rack, where, evidently, they had just met for the first time. In my own cubicle, where I could summon no interest in my try-on selections, I eavesdropped shamelessly.

A distraught voice mumbled something I couldn't quite catch about the size of the dress she was trying on.

"Sometimes I'm a size 4, sometimes I'm a size 16," a kindly voice answered. And then the kindly voice almost groaned. "But ooh, girl, you've *got* to buy that."

"You're the best thing that has happened to me," said the sad voice, sniffling.

"And why is that?" asked the fountain of light.

"Pray for me tonight," her new friend said, crying openly now. And then she revealed the details of too grand investments that had gone sour, leaving her worrying about paying her bills.

"My pastor says pray *now*," the fountain of light said, "don't wait until tonight." And they prayed: "Thank you Jesus for letting me find this dress."

~

Though I often fail to find what it is I need in stores, I am still moved by their warm light, which beckons like the yellow glow of lamps visible through other people's closed lace curtains. I am still moved by merchandise, tawdry, or tasteful, or good-tasting, its easy promise; the Christmas paper at 50% off glitters for me; the magenta rayon-lace panties I saw a woman holding up and scrutinizing at K-Mart do have a certain allure; hybrid fruit at the yuppie supermarket makes my mouth water—pear-apple, is it crisp as an apple, sweet as a pear? Late capitalist solace: you go into the warmth, hand over a few coins, and bring something out in a bag. Sometimes I find myself standing alone at twilight in the parking lot outside a discount store where I buy fruits and vegetables my mother would have considered "beautiful," bags from my shopping cart in my arms, not getting into my car. Newspapers and city grit blow against my ankles in the California desert wind, the same newspapers and grit as on Bronx streets, the evening is still tender blue, the yellow street lamps just on, and I am thinking, with bags in hand, of that moment of our bringing packages home, of bursting in the door with our new wares to exhibit, whether delights for the stomach or the eyes.

So, it was with a sense of memory poignantly sweet that I responded to a heavyset woman's slightly hesitant request as I thumbed listlessly through some blouses near the dressing room at a local department store this spring. "Excuse me," she said as she emerged from the dressing room, "Would you mind giving me a second opinion?"

Oh, it's as weighty as what you get from the doctor, that I know. When the daughter had summoned her mom to look, I'd already caught a glimpse: a lissome body in an ice-blue satin prom gown with spaghetti straps, a bandeau across the small breasts, an extraordinary fit. "No, not at all," I said, happy I looked kind enough to be asked.

And now the daughter, beckoned out by the mother who really knows, and whose hesitation is already almost a celebration. The daughter with shoulders hunched a little as if to dim the glow of her beauty, smiling shyly beneath her lowered head and eyes, and looking like Daphne just turned back from a laurel tree.

And I'm saying in a rush, delighted to give my benediction and my testimony, "she's stunning, it's stunning, I don't care what anybody says, you've *got* to buy it."

Decorum: An Immigrant Elegy

I.

In your closet a declension:

a few expensive knits in cleaner's plastic
two tailored jackets
a blouse of navy dotted swiss
a pedal pusher outfit
faded house dresses
a red sweater I outgrew
in 9th grade

and 40 years of shoes
in boxes
in style
then out
in style
then out
in style again

but easiest to reach
my too large crumpled dingy
sweats, borrowed for rehab,
hung up by Poppa.

I put my head inside
your everyday wool coat.
In one pocket
      tissues.
In the other pocket
      tissues
        and a coupon.

Saved, untouched,
in your bureau drawer,
the "too fancy" bedjacket
sent by your sister-in-law,
also, a torn pajama bottom—
elastic waist pinned to size—
a brushed nylon nightgown
worn to gauze,
an envelope of girdle garters.

II.

Told you'd soon be going down for surgery
on the hip you broke after your second stroke,
you asked me "what should I wear"
and planned "the gabardine pants."

"Going down" must have kept a little fragrance
of meeting an occasion—
a descent in a New York apartment elevator
into the formal street.

III

I said "Jewish" and "closed."
I said "No, we have no shroud,"
and the funeral director in your adopted town
asked for your clothes.

I thought of arraying you, mother,
in your knit with the golden braid—
as if you had gotten to the grand-niece's wedding,
or the bar mitzvah your California grandson
never had—

or at least in the useless bedjacket.

But the you in me ("Who *needs* it!")
wouldn't let me give that much
to Death.

So you lie in your clean velour robe
with the broken zipper pinned, hospital
slippers, and a soft cotton
nightgown I never wore, not liking the color,
and your clothes adorn the backs
of unknown ladies, "4 petite,"

and I, your neat, good, thrifty daughter
cross "Learn to give insulin"
off my list, and keep only:

the Sabbath prayer in transliterated Hebrew you cut from a circular,
your little card with the Mourner's Kaddish,
which I found in the inner pocket
of one of your good-as-new
old purses.

The Pregnant Body

Spring 1970. I am eight and a half months pregnant, waiting in an uncomfortable molded plastic chair for a pre-natal appointment at an HMO near my new home in Southern California where my husband has taken his first academic job as an Assistant Professor of Anthropology. The child to be is unreal, though imminent; my almost completed PhD dissertation in English that I wish were completed and behind me is all too real. In any case, I am suddenly a "faculty wife" in a precipitously declining academic job market. The luck of the OB appointment draw today seems to be the only woman on staff. The previous luck of the draw had included the not unlikable darkly humorous doc who held a cigarette in his mouth and dropped the ash on the none-too-clean examining room floor. He said: "Stopping smoking might be more of a shock to your pregnant body than continuing to smoke."

The luck of the draw had also included the head of OB-GYN. I asked him about the side effects of spinal anesthesia. He said: "Some people drop dead."

~

"Gracious living" abided in my dorm at Smith, during my undergraduate years on scholarship in the early 60s, and many of the girls, preparing for wifedom, read *The Joy of Cooking* in their beds at night. An intense former student, married (or was she divorced?) and in grad school, gave a talk about marriage and graduate study for the seniors planning further education. She was a catastrophic thinker, brow furrowed with angst, ready to sacrifice the subordinate's career to the cause of inbred, gendered aptitudes. She asked, rhetorically, "Who will make the coffee on the day both of your dissertations are due?"

At my "girls' school," I sought out a woman professor, who

had a husband and family as well as a career, to supervise my senior thesis. I had to change my subject from Donne and Herbert to Gerard Manley Hopkins to find one. (The woman Lecturer in seventeenth-century was single.) A child answered, when, prospectus in hand, I knocked on the door of my Victorianist's house, where she lived with her history professor husband.

"Do you wish to see my mother or my father?" the little girl asked. She wore only a bedraggled slip with holes in the hem. Holy imperfection! No difficulties about coffee brewing in that house, I presumed.

A sympathetic English professor at my college arranged a telephone conversation to facilitate my late but not unimpressive application to a West Coast grad school (my fiancé and I had been accepted at grad schools on opposite coasts). The professor at my not yet grad school to which my husband had already been admitted was being asked to show an iota of understanding about the bind a couple was in. "We don't provide conveniences for young marrieds!" he said on the phone. But I was, eventually, accepted.

I had my initial interview with the Graduate Advisor soon after my husband and I arrived.

"I hope you're not one of those women who are going to have babies," he said.

"I hope my plumbing is in good order," I said. (Feisty once.)

One of the two new women hires joining the all-male English Department arrived heavily pregnant and was observed pulling herself hand over hand up the stairs in the fall of 1964. "She kept *that* well-hidden," some second-year women students who'd heard her presentation in the spring chuckled. With a certain admiration for a necessary feat.

To explain the way dissertation fellowships had been awarded, the Dean of Humanities said, "Only nuns and maiden ladies are 'good risks.'" A number of statistically skilled spouses including mine said "Not true!" and proved it with ample evidence. (The policy was adjusted.)

~

Oh, it was a whirl to be young, newly married, in grad school with great expectations, though we had no money our first year and ate spaghetti without the sauce, though we had some colossal fights under the lovely stone arches on the way to our first grad classes of the day, and I smoked too much because it helped me to study, and there was a strange professor who nearly gave me a nervous breakdown—a famous one who failed people who had the temerity to love Dylan Thomas and other disapproved authors I learned to stay away from.

It was a whirl to accompany my husband to exotic West Africa for his PhD field work, having happily internalized the cultural relativism of his discipline (our marriage a marriage of intellectual exchange), and on the way to meet friends in England, world travelers like ourselves, then to come back with my husband—his field work completed—for my turn to research my own dissertation at an august English library (one couple, two tax-free fellowships, almost rich!), to walk in the golden-hued city of Oxford, to rub brasses at Cotswold churches. I felt like a sophisticated world citizen, though, at the Oxford college I was affiliated with while on my dissertation fellowship, my "maiden lady" supervisor—her decency not withstanding—never failed to correct my American and New York pronunciation, and the English were so chilly, the only place we could socialize was the Commonwealth Club where we danced the "high-life" with so much more friendly West Africans, and our flat near Oxford was so cold my parents couldn't bear to stay in it and went downtown to a hotel with central heating, even though they were so desperate to see us after close to two years, they'd flown

The author and her husband, Legon, Accra, Ghana. 1967.

across the Atlantic at a hefty cost.

My young life felt—at the very moment of living it—like a play in which I was one of the highly individual characters, glorying in my uniqueness, and then, fairly quickly, it no longer did. Seven months pregnant, jobless and dwindling by degrees into that faculty wife, I went to an interview for a teaching position conducted by a panel of men at a state school. I made not-so-stately progress into the room, like a heavily laden curved-prowed (not so proud) vessel. They all stared at my belly as if it were a cancer. Thinking back on that experience, I want to take completely out of context and adjust some lines by Mary Oliver and call the poem "The Pregnant Body":

> and every [woman]
> no matter what [her]
> name is, is
> nameless now.

At a party hosted by a member of my husband's department, a linguist's wife said: "You are a cow if you don't have natural childbirth." Counter-intuitive?

The La Leche people said breastfeeding was holy. But I still didn't know whether I was going to nurse or bottle-feed. Did bottle-feeding really mean sterilizing bottles in one of those jam-making pots with the wire basket? I hadn't researched this area yet, though my baby was due in two weeks. Finally put into a room by a nurse for that last pre-natal appointment at eight and a half months, I lay on the examining table in my hospital gown clutching that question in my mind.

Dr. N. barely nodded at me when she swept in, exuding no-nonsense briskness. Maybe she was the medical equivalent of Hillary Clinton on foreign policy, proving she was as tough as the guys.

"I have a few questions," I whispered, as she started her examination, "for when you're finished." Ever the patient patient.

"Do you always have questions," she said.

"Yes, I do," I said, in a very unfeisty voice.

She ignored me, finished the examination, snapped off her gloves and moved to the sink to wash her hands, clearly ready to dismiss me. I don't remember how I got off the examining table. I doubt a hand was proffered. I fumbled for my clothes. She turned and left the room.

Still pulling the stretch panel of my maternity pants over my swollen belly, I followed her down the hall, further chilled by my glimpse through the open door of her office of the Gothic letters on her desk nameplate (for the very reason that my father's family—with the exception of his murdered older sister, her husband, and children—had successfully escaped Hitler's Germany; it was a long time before I traveled to Berlin and found that I liked it). Maybe Dr. N.'s own medical training had been of the Nazi-ish variety.

"Dr. N! I just need to know if I have to sterilize—" I urgently blurted.

S-T-E-R-I-L-I-Z-E reached her ears as she neared the doors marked NO ENTRY at the end of the hall. "You immoral woman," she shouted, "not yet 30 years old and you want your tubes tied?"

I imagined fumes issuing from the back of her head, as she launched herself into a tirade against the tying off of Fallopian tubes. "Bottles, not tubes," I kept saying, as clearly as I could. "Bottles! NOT tubes!"

The sound waves were agonizingly slow. She reached the door, then abruptly turned towards me again, on her heel. "In any case, I am NOT a pediatrician. I AM AN OBSTETRICIAN," she said through gritted teeth, "and I have no idea how you can get this information." Then she turned a final time with seeming military precision and swung through the doors.

~

Luck of the draw: Dr. N. was on duty, contending for the Oscar for her role in *Coldness and Condescension* when my husband and I came into the hospital sixteen days later, at the beginning of my 26-hour labor with my first child. I used my Lamaze breathing during contractions until I was 6 centimeters dilated.

"If you keep that up, you'll hyperventilate," said Dr. N.

The peaks of contractions and the valleys in-between began to blur. I needed some relief. Yet I couldn't entirely give up the idea of natural childbirth. And I didn't want to be cowed.

A triumphant Dr. N., ready to administer a dose of scopolamine, made very clear that this was a decision fork; if I received the medication, a medicated delivery would follow, however many hours ahead; my husband—useful coach and supporter—would immediately be dismissed from the labor room. We couldn't understand why some relief, Demerol, perhaps, could not be combined with a wait-and-see approach. Or why my husband had to leave, especially since hardly any staff dropped in, in any case. We argued.

"I am not a halfway woman," said Dr. N. "I am a doctor."

Almost slaphappy with solidarity, exhaustion, and frustration, we said, "We're doctors, too."

Scopolamine was administered; the bars of my bed went up with an institutional clang; my husband was ushered out; I moved into a restless fog from which I abruptly wakened at intervals to increasingly ungovernable pain; Dr. N. disappeared (dereliction of duty?); the nurse very quickly invited my helpful husband back in. Eventually, the darkly humorous obstetrician came on and told me we needed to get the show on the road: spinal, baby that needed to come out, happy ending.

~

How real our acculturation is at any moment in history! Oh you beautiful young mommies of today, baring your baby bumps or basketballs in string bikinis, reveling in spandex leggings with stretchy t-shirts on top, showing off your outie belly buttons, having water births at home with doulas, never having had to wear a maternity sack with a large bow across the breasts, or be guilty of "job-interviewing-while-pregnant." Oh Kelly Clarkson on the *American Idol* finale singing your heart out in your glam heels and tight black dress, revealing just how close you are to your due date, earthily flaunting your pregnant belly with little belly jerks in time to the music—Let me remind you all how it was.

~

Four years after my son was born, and by then, totally uncowed, I went through labor and the delivery of my daughter with the help of a perfectly trained Lamaze nurse who said, "Good job, good job, keep panting, okay NOW, PUSH!" Nevertheless, driving home from that long ago pre-natal appointment I had endured alone with the vicious Dr. N., I was shell-shocked, weeping, wounded, rather than furious and indignant, as I should have been. But the anger built after our son's birth. A team of two, my husband and I wrote to that very OB-GYN head ("some people drop dead"), and got a letter back thanking us for our "thoughtful analysis of the deficiencies in our obstetrical department, both in our method of delivery of care and in the personalities of our physicians and nursing staffs." If those were ironic words, he had to chew and swallow them, before long.

Noblesse Oblige

I was well-married as Miranda
to Ferdinand, zippy as Rosalind
in Arden, ponytailed like a kid,
at my first MLA in 1971, when the handsome
professor of Middle English lit
who'd taken to saying in class,
Feel free to call me Rick! (was he
newly entering the late '60s zeitgeist?) invited me
to his room on some job search
pretext. Assuming concern
tantamount to my own
ambitions, I went, not overly
suspicious, and watched while he,
obvious as an undergraduate
cribber, poured more Scotch
than I might drink in a month
of grad student dinners. But his lips when he
kissed me descended softly
as dewe in Aprille
that falleth on the flowr—their pressure
subtle as the most deft irony.
I helplessly savored
their touch, then begged off,
murmuring something earnest
about loyalty. He asked, *Are you*
sure? then let me go,
then said—as my heart fell through all
the stories of myself like an elevator
out of control—*I'll* still *write you*
a good letter for that job.

Medical Management of High Maintenance Mom

My mother sighed heavily down onto the crinkling paper, telling the doctor apologetically that she wasn't going to mention it, but she had been feeling *eppes farmahtert* of late. She underplayed the "tired" and failed to mention the "whooshing" sound in her head she'd described to me in the car; you could get into a whole tsimmes with doctors if you didn't watch out—the blood tests, those scans, and God forbid, hospital admission and the operating table.

It was only the third or fourth time I had accompanied her to her doctor's appointment since she and my father had moved to my inland Southern California town from New Rochelle, New York some eight years before, when they were in their seventies. My father—usually the "strong one" in her estimate, and her sometimes reluctant medical manager—was at home with bronchitis. My mother had never learned to drive, and even if she had, she would normally have insisted on his presence in the examining room. In the last year or so, she lobbied for a triumvirate that included me, her daughter and only child, the "educated" interlocutor. From my first visit, Dr. B., her "diabetes man," practically swept me in; his nurse always brought an extra chair.

"Maybe it's just my age," my mother was saying, smiling disarmingly, and making her knee jerk as Dr. B. hit it with his little metal hammer. It was as if she expected him to say, "Oh eighty's young these days."

But he didn't. He said "Relax, please," sending me the briefest look of bemusement and readiness to ask for help. I got up and placed my hand on her bird-fragile shoulder blades. Now, trying out a new way of passing the test, my mother held her knee rigid when the doctor tapped it again with the little hammer. "No,

No, Mrs. Z.," he almost chuckled, "*Relax*." He adjusted his stethoscope in his ears, and I sat down again. He was examining her in the same poker-faced way he always did, which could mean that he'd heeded what she said, or ignored it.

"*Somewhat* tired," my mother was muttering again, apparently unable to bear the suspense. "As I was telling my daughter, Dr. B. has a way of fixing me up. Wasn't I, Judy?" Pointed look at me. Sudden dazzling smile at Dr. B. "A little more insulin, a little less insulin … He's *good*."

Ah, ingratiation! For my immigrant parents—especially for my mother—it was something like a savings account into which one put money against the nasty turns of cold fate. She made regular deposits in all weathers. The funny thing was how well it worked, for the most part (however acutely embarrassing for me). My parents were well liked; they seemed to get concerned service. In any event, it was personalized service. They seemed to recreate around them the village-like corner of the provincial Bronx in which I grew up, where all the shopkeepers were known by name.

"*Really* good," my mother was saying.

"Shh, shh," said Dr. B., smiling, waggling his free index finger back and forth as he listened to her chest.

~

Those who know Canter's restaurant on Fairfax Avenue in L.A. know you enter a time warp when you go there. Some of the waiters stoop and shuffle, and little grey-haired old ladies wearing stockings rolled up at the knees shtup their mouths full of chopped liver on rye, their heads bent low over their plates. Culturally—if not religiously, in any technical sense—my mother was a time-warp within such a time warp. Canter's was seriously out of her ken. It's open on Friday night and Saturday, and it sells ham along with the brisket. My mother was like a fossil from the late Yiddish Paleolithic, revivified by some miraculous process, dropped into suburban SoCal and a Reform congregation, without recognizing that she was no longer in the Bronx or New Rochelle.

She and my dad, with their still thick accents, were old world icons at their temple, where the congregation seemed to be 80% over sixty-five, 10% converts and 10% New Agers, and where guitar music figured prominently in the service; they were an adorable ethnic kewpie doll couple. Sometimes I felt the temple could have miniaturized them, cast them in sugar and sold them as quaint ornaments for wedding cakes. Her miniature would have been outfitted in a long-sleeved high-necked dress, nylon stockings with seams, and a bouffant black wig; his would have had a beard down to his chest, side-curls, and a huge fur hat (even though they never were Hasids): SoCal suburb by way of New York, by way of Lemberg and Duisburg, by way of *Fiddler on the Roof*. Their arms would be hinged at the elbow, and he would be graciously holding hers, as in their formal wedding portrait of 1939—though their relationship at home was sometimes far from gracious.

~

The stethoscope part of the exam seemed to be going on longer than usual. Huh, what was this? In a level tone my mother was not picking up on, Dr. B. was murmuring something about "her heart, an arrhythmia, possibly asymptomatic, or, perhaps, something more serious, see the cardiologist?" Was this the nasty turn? As my mother would say, my heart gave a *kuh-nock*. They had been relatively lucky, so I had been as well. They were *two* and the reluctant medical manager was my dad, seven years younger; neither had been hospitalized for a very long time. Previous health crises—in which I had been involved via extensive phone conversations with my parents, calls to their doctors, the occasional extended New Rochelle visit—seemed rare interruptions in the steady routines of their home. They'd somehow never been seriously ill at the same time. At their riper and more fragile ages, the fatal disruption loomed ahead.

We took the elevator to the lab in the hospital basement for the blood work Dr. B. wanted done, *stat*, which he would send directly on to Dr. L., the cardiologist. On the way down, my mother cogitated about which of her ailments she was going to pay attention to this time. The blood sugar, she'd watch. *Of course.* It was rising a bit, but nothing alarming yet. "Let's make an appointment with the cardiologist," I said, "it's about time for a checkup." I could have said "How about a bite of this nice spinach?"

"Once you start with those cardio people you never finish," my mother said.

I was probably more worried about unbounded expanses of time than she was. I was a university lecturer, rather than the "English professor" my mother concocted. I always felt the pressure of grading and planning for classes during the hours I wasn't teaching, not to mention the need to make time for the writing required to snag a better job.

I walked the corridor while my mother had her blood drawn, having slipped out when the lab tech said, "She'll be done in a jiffy," and before my mother could muster the words to invite me in, in her oddly gay manner, as if for coffee and cake. There was a rack of educational pamphlets. *How to Deal with Peptic Ulcers*, *Exercises for the Back*, *Common Intestinal Disorders*, *Watching your Weight*. The pamphlet on *Coping with Death* had the same cute stick figures—sad mouths and tears dripping down their flat cheeks. Suddenly I felt in need of a middle generation between myself and the mother who was nearly twice my age, a need of some parents for me, or some other children for my mother and father, who could take up the slack. I fantasized that my children—my son graduated from college and working in San Francisco, my daughter just starting college up North—would rush into taking charge of the grandparents who had showered their childhoods with visits from UPS, "the present man." I knew my husband would eventually listen, try to analyze the situation, make suggestions, and even accompany me in a crisis, but he didn't do doctor's appointments. I fantasized stoic Midwestern parents who quietly took care of themselves when they had ailments—the kind who wrote longhand letters to their coastal daughter to inform her that one or the other had just nicely recovered from surgery.

We headed out the double glass doors into the overcast late November day. The wind, beginning to have a raw edge, was kicking up in the parking lot, lifting the still warm humid smell of the pavement to our noses. My mother, head bent against it, coughed and listed towards her good leg. "A pleasure," she sighed, as I knew she would, when she sank into the soft warmth of the passenger seat; she sounded like someone who had just relieved herself after a long ride without a bathroom stop.

"Are you sure you don't want to come to the Oneg next Friday night?" she asked, waking up from a doze or a thought-cloud, after we'd driven a few blocks.

"No thanks, Mom," I said. I suppressed "Are you *kidding*?" I was planning on waiting at least until retirement, or never, to join her temple. Really, my future was more likely to include bench pressing than *bentching*. When I got old, I thought I'd go to the Fit Forever aerobics classes at the gym. I'd wandered into the room once, looking for some of the free weights they kept there, and was hit on by a liver-spotted specimen of old-age spunk. It did occur to me that those retiree temple members, after cutting out the coupons from the Sunday paper and arranging the maraschino cherry halves on hubby's vanilla pudding might have a little time on their hands to take a friend to the occasional doctor's appointment, if I got into a pinch. But, as a nonmember who chalked up only the rare visit, I felt awkward about asking.

"You know my friend Bea?" my mother was saying. I thought I recognized the name—the one who was almost blind? No chauffeur there. "Well,"—my mother sounded a little tight-lipped because I'd nixed the Oneg—"she used to believe in evolution. But she took some courses and now she's back with God."

Intellectually, my mother could sound like the Christian right wing. I glanced over at her dry dyed-black hair, her barely-there eyebrows, her thin mouth and crinkled cheeks. Though I knew her hearing was poor, her vision getting worse, and she couldn't walk very far without pain, she had still *looked* the same for decades. *Okay,* I thought, getting my bearings after the dosage of indirection. We'll get the results of the tests and we'll figure out the next step.

She erupted again from her thought-cloud after we got on the freeway. "He won't let me touch him. He won't tell me if he's got a fever."

Aha. It had only been a matter of time.

"He says, 'If I die, I die. You're just worried about someone to take care of you.'"

It was not an uncompelling argument.

She opened her purse and thrust a torn envelope at me. "Call his doctor," she said.

Speeding along the freeway, I thrust the envelope aside with my right hand. She shrugged slightly, and placed it deliberately on top of her purse in her lap.

"Maybe after Daddy gets better," she muttered. "I don't think I'll tell Dr. B. about the whooshing sound in my head. Maybe after Daddy gets better."

A minute later, her left hand, clutching the envelope, swung out again, practically across my face. "Daddy wants you to call," she said shamelessly.

When we pulled into the garage under their apartment, I took the envelope from her with a sigh. *Karottes, Lettes, Zelery, Brokely, Dr. S. 603-7986*: all in her wavery European hand. Teetering slightly in her heels, my mother fiddled with the door key. The drizzle had turned her hair wild. "Sam? SamMY?" she called, as we entered.

There was a strong, familiar smell of camphor and furniture polish, with undercurrents of Lysol, garlic, and onions. I heard the red kettle they'd had as long as I could remember bubbling weakly on the electric burner as we passed the kitchen. On the counter next to it was the ancient sugar bowl—now used for Sweet'N Low—that I had painted with the letters "M-O-M" enclosed in a flowering heart, per her suggestion, in grade school. There was something weirdly goose-bump inciting about entering my parents' domestic space, with its antimacassars, its bureau scarves, the paper doilies under the potted philoden-drons, the small silk throw pillow placed precisely at either end of the brocade sofa. My mother had waited for me outside for her ride that morning out of a concern with "contagion" she'd apparently forgotten when we got back. I hadn't been inside their apartment since we'd picked them up for dinner in Oc-tober. I felt like I was inside a large dollhouse, but it wasn't really unpleasant. The rain was pattering steadily outside now.

My mother called out "Judy!" from the bedroom where she'd immediately gone. I followed her down the hall, inhaling Cash-mere Bouquet (the bathroom) and Lemon Pledge (the guest room). Dad lay with the covers pulled up to his chin; his flushed cheeks were covered with white stubble. He opened one grey eye.

"So?" he said, directly to me.

"So, I'll live," my mother said to the air, meaning *no thanks to you* and *for all you care* and *in spite of what you might have hoped. Kids. Kids.*

"Nothing out of the ordinary," she finished. *You hope*, I

thought. She was eyeing his dirty white terrycloth robe which was draped over the bedpost.

"What did I tell you," he said. "Mind over matter."

Mother couldn't see me; I shook my head, frowning, eyes down.

With some difficulty, she yanked the robe off the post and placed it, with deliberation, on the clothes tree near the window.

"I can't reach it there," Dad tried to shout, then broke into a croaking cough.

"See," mother said pointedly to me. She began to lift the used tissues from Dad's night table and to neatly arrange the tissue box, cough drops, Tylenol, water glass, teacup.

"I called my doctor," Dad whispered conspiratorially. Mom was in the bathroom washing the thermometer she'd whisked off the night table which she'd squinted at but been unable to read.

"He called in a new prescription to the drugstore," Dad forced a whisper again, his voice squeaking randomly, like wind in a flue. He looked up at me, eyebrows raised.

"What did her doctor really say?" he whispered. *Kids!*

~

Compared to dealing with my parents, picking up the new antibiotic for Dad and making an appointment with the cardiologist for Mom was clean work. "Such concern!" my mother said when I called her afterwards to give her the time. "You're a living doll. But you know—doctors don't always know everything."

The next afternoon, a day before her "squeezed-in" appointment, Dad rang me in my tiny shared office. Mom had been acting "a little peculiar." Maybe she needed some, uh, "supervision." When he tried to give her her diabetes pill a little while before, she had spit it out. "I can take care of myself," she'd said, waving him away, "as if you cared." Then she fell asleep. He was worried about her insulin, too, didn't think she'd taken it. But when he brought her the cartridge syringe and shook her awake, "Oh *no*," she said. "I'm not going to give you the chance."

"Nice, huh," he said, and broke into a fit of coughing.

I called Dr. B. He wanted my mother at the hospital, *stat*. I scribbled a note for my office door.

"I feel okay," my mother said when I buckled her in. "A little … *light*, that's all."

"Did you take all your medicine today, your Diabeta—?"

"*Of course* I did," she said. "I *think* I did."

~

"Now you'll give that nice big purse to your daughter, won't you," said the clerk at hospital admissions. The diabetes man had phoned ahead.

"She's coming with me," my mother said. And I was.

"How do you like *that*?" she said after they wheeled her up to the diabetes ward, gave me her clothes, put her in her hospital gown, slapped the leads on for her first EKG. "What a surprise."

"Hmm," the nurse who pulled the tape off the machine was saying, quite audibly.

"How do you like *that*?" my mother repeated. I could almost understand why her temple found her "adorable."

A tall, heavyset nurse came in, put a paper-covered thermometer in Mom's mouth, put a blood pressure cuff on her skinny arm and held on to her wrist. Her brow furrowed as she took Mom's blood pressure and measured her pulse. She took the cuff off Mom's arm, then pricked her finger with an instrument from a kit.

"I have the little pink pills for that," my mother said. "They're in my purse."

"Isn't she a cutie," the nurse said. She was dark-haired and had a slight Spanish accent.

"I'd like to be home in time to watch *L.A. Law*," my mother said.

"You can watch it here, right in your own bed!" the nurse said. "Just not too loud." She pointed to the speaker for the TV behind mother's head, and then to the neighboring bed around which the curtains had been drawn.

The nurse wheeled in an IV stand, started an IV on mother's left hand, then left. My mother squeezed shut her left eye, then opened it and looked blankly at the plastic bag hanging above her head.

A doctor in a white coat came in, said he was the cardiologist on duty, patted mother's hand, muttered something about blood gasses and getting back to us later.

The dark-haired nurse came back in, tied a rubber tourniquet around Mother's right arm, and started to draw her blood.

Mother scrunched up her mouth. "Such a big needle!" she said, turning her face away. I turned away too. The tourniquet came off with a *thwack*. "I hope I'm home in time for Tom Brokaw. You like him, too, don't you," she said to the nurse.

She was out and back in a moment with an oxygen cart; she adjusted the transparent tubing under Mother's nostrils.

"This'll make you feel good," she said.

"I feel good now," Mother said.

The nurse left. It was quiet for a few moments.

"You should go home," Mother said. "You have work to do. You should go home." Then she swung her legs over the side of the bed, leaned on the elbow of the IV hand, and stood up. The oxygen tubing fell out of her nostrils.

"What *is* this?" she said. "What *is* this?"

"Here," I said, "it goes like this." Her cheeks were papery under my fingers as I placed the little prongs under her nostrils. One dripped clear mucous.

"What *is* this?" she said, shaking her head like a dog with a foxtail in its ear.

She shook the robe we'd brought out of her plastic shopping bag, refolded it carefully, placed it on the back of the chair near the bed, changed her mind, tried to walk around the bed to the other side where there was a metal stand with a single drawer. The IV tubing caught her up short. "What *IS* this?" she said. I tried to show her that she could walk with the IV stand, but move her arm only so far as the leash would let her; I offered to put the robe in the drawer for her. But she didn't want to play the patient "at home." She put the robe back in the shopping bag and stood by the side of the bed.

"I have an idea," she said. She bent down to pick up her purse. "They must have a cafeteria. Let's go for coffee." The oxygen tubing popped from her nostrils again. Angrily, she felt around her neck and pulled it over her head.

"Mom," I said, "*what* are you doing?"

The tall, dark-haired nurse came by with the afternoon's ration of pills in a little cup.

"Why don't you take a rest, sweetie pie," the nurse said. "Uh-oh, where's your oxygen?"

"Rest I get enough of," my mother said. Frowning, she raised her chin so the oxygen necklace could go around her again.

"There's no pink pills here," my mother said, looking into the cup. "I'd better get them out of my purse."

"Isn't she a cutie. Love that accent," the nurse said. "Where's she from? No, honey," she said, turning towards my mother, "you take ours here."

Her invisible roommate's bedside phone rang. My mother looked startled, jerked her head around, searching for the source of the sound.

The dietician dropped off the dinner request cards.

"I think I'd better slip out and call Dad," I murmured.

"When is he coming?" she said. She squinted at the yellow paper requesting her meal choices. I handed her her glasses from the bed tray.

When the phone at her own bedside table rang, she looked startled again. Her head swiveled like a periscope. Finally, she picked up the receiver with ginger fingers.

"Danny, my love!" she said. I knew my son was going to call home about some job-related tax questions; he must have gotten the news.

"How is school?"

"Don't worry, sweetheart, Grandma's going to be out of here in a jiffy!"

"Of course you do, my angel, of course you do." She hung up before I could catch her.

"I can't make this out," she said, quite calmly, handing the yellow paper to me. She laboriously swallowed the pills, one at a time, with the water the nurse had fetched.

"Creamed chipped beef with string beans, or seafood salad," I read with a sinking heart.

"I can't eat this," she said.

"My mother observes the Jewish dietary laws," I said to the nurse.

She looked puzzled.

"She doesn't eat certain foods, like meat— Are you Catholic, by any chance?" I asked, knowing the example I had in mind wouldn't work.

"There's seafood," said the nurse. "I'm Christian," she said.

I began to imagine a glorified version of the New York hospital my mother had thyroid surgery in ten years before, a place where she would not be the anomaly she was here and now in suburban SoCal. In my hospital, many of the doctors would look like prospective grandsons-in-law (or second husbands for me if the never-approved-one I had didn't work out). They would chuck her under her chin and make her promise to bring some of that good stuffed helzel when she got well. The nurses would kvel about their own accomplished sons and nephews and commiserate about daughters who didn't enjoy the special bond of watching their mother's blood being drawn. My hospital would have catered coffee and Danish at all hours of the night and day for patients and guests, piped-in klezmer music, worry rooms instead of chapels, grandchildren for hire, and its manual would be *The Indirection Guidebook.*

"No, no, no!" my mother was saying. She prodded my side with her elbow with surprising strength and shot me a fierce look. "I'm *vegetarian. You* know that!" She looked at the inside of the other elbow, bruised purple and yellow from the drawing of blood. "Daddy should see this," she said sternly. "When is he coming?"

"Uh, be right back," I said.

~

I had to go to the pay phone in the corridor outside the ward. I walked by the rooms, avoiding looking in, hearing the breathing of equipment, the babble of many TVs. In one room someone weakly yelled, *Help. Please help me. Help*, like an exhausted swimmer losing his battle against a riptide. I recognized the on-duty cardiologist coming out of another room, his head in a chart.

"Can you talk to me for a minute?" I asked.

He looked up blankly.

"I'm Mrs. Z.'s daughter."

"Oh. Yes."

"There's nothing too remarkable there. At least, I don't think. She's definitely got an arrhythmia—don't know if that explains the symptoms that brought her in here, though. Hmm. It's sort of asymptomatic—but yes, it's there. We kind of look at it in context. Probably controllable with medication—we're starting that now. Meanwhile we'll rule out other possibilities."

~

"So," my father said, on the phone.

"The cardiologist here says she's got some kind of arrhythmia—just like the diabetes guy thought on Tuesday." Two judgments had more of an empirical ring.

"And what is that exactly?"

"I guess it means her heart skips beats."

"Wait a minute," my father said. A paroxysm of coughing, slightly muffled, as if with a handkerchief over the receiver to protect me from germs.

I promised I'd take him to see Dr. S. in the morning.

"And how is she?" He had recovered his breath.

I lowballed it. "Uh, okay I guess. Not happy about being here. Anything you want me to tell her?" I asked hopefully.

~

When I got back to the room, my mother stood hauling up the sheet with both hands so it covered the pillow. She took the white hospital blanket that had been folded at the bottom of the bed and tried to shake it out.

"Mother," I said, "what are you doing"?

"I need to make the bed," she said. She carefully brought a few inches of sheet over the edge of the blanket, smoothed it down, smoothed down as much as she could reach of the rest of the blanket. "There," she said, "that's better." There was a cup with a trickle of juice and an opened package of crackers on her bed tray from the snack they'd given her. She gathered these up and dropped them in the plastic wastebasket; then she brushed the crumbs off the tray onto the floor. I looked away.

The dark-haired nurse popped her head in. "Naughty, naughty, Mrs. Z." She wagged her finger. "We really don't like all that good oxygen, do we?" Mother scowled as the nurse put the transparent tubing under her nostrils again.

"Now I'm just going to stay for a while and see that you get real calm. We'll see if there's anything nice on TV." She turned on the set and adjusted the speaker behind mother's head. Then she sat down. "We'll just have a little look-see," she said.

"Do I hear a radio? Is there a radio in here?" Mother said, turning her head away from the TV towards the speakers behind her. She sat stiffly, not leaning back, her legs straight out in front of her on the made bed.

"I guess the hospital's really strange for her," I said to the nurse, half apology, half plea.

"Hospitals aren't *that* strange," she smiled. She got up, cranked up the back of the bed for Mother to lean back against, pulled the top sheet and blanket from under Mother's legs and covered her with them, tucking the blanket ends firmly under the mattress. "Now that's a little better," she said to Mother. I felt like picking up the nurse and depositing her in a mock-up stage set—*General Hospital* in Disneyland, where she would become silent as cardboard.

"Where *is* she from?" she asked, sitting down again.

"She was born in Austria," I said, fudging a bunch of complexity. But she's been in America for over 60 years."

"Still, her roots are there," she said. She glanced over at my mother again. "She *is* kind of cute."

"Do you hear singing?" Mother said. "Is Danny here? Is that who's singing?" She looked at me with daft charm, as if I'd prepared a surprise.

"No, Dan's in San Francisco," I said.

"But I hear him!" she said. She bent over and peered under the bed. "Are you sure he's not here?" she asked, still smiling.

"Mother!" I said.

"Not all our elderly manage to simply live and die," the nurse said softly. She tipped her head. "Some of them, unfortunately, decline."

~

It was seven or so when I left the hospital, chilly and winter-dark. I stopped at the supermarket to buy my father some prepared food—some soups that had the "kosher" mark because I feared defiling my mother's household. At the apartment I knocked, then opened the door with my key and called, "Dad?"

"I can't sleep in our bed," he said. "But I can't sleep here either." He had made up a bed for himself on the living room couch in front of the TV where he sat in his sweatpants and jacket.

"How is she?"

"Restless," I said.

"Mm-hmm." Dad said. "There was something she could eat?"

"She sniffed at the soy burger and made a face at the dishwater coffee, but she ate a few bites and took a few sips."

"That's good," he said.

"And you?" I said. "What are you going to eat?" I showed him the cans I had bought.

He turned them over listlessly. "Maybe later," he said. "I don't have much of an appetite."

"Let me make you some more tea," I said.

I went into the bedroom to get his cup. The bed was neatly made with the quilted bedspread. Dad's white terry robe was hanging, its belt neatly tied, on the clothes tree. On the night table the tissue box, cough drops, Tylenol, a clean water glass, and the new antibiotic Dr. S. had prescribed were lined up with mathematical precision.

In the kitchen I set the red kettle to boil, found a lemon, and put the cup, a lemon slice and the Sweet'N Low "M-O-M" bowl on a tray.

~

It was raining hard again when I got home, exhausted. Rare weather for a California winter, even if we needed it. "How many more days is it going to do this?" I asked my husband, after I'd given him an update. I was thinking that some dry weather might help my dad lick the bronchitis.

"Thirty-seven," he said, ruefully.

~

When I took Dad to see him the next morning, Dr. S. actually thought the bronchitis was coming around with the new medicine. The thing to watch out for was pneumonia. He recommended a nutritional drink which came in flavors such as Rich Fudge and Creamy Butterscotch. Was Dad going to go home now? Perhaps his wife would try to fix a particularly tempting light meal?

"My wife is in the hospital," Dad said.

"Nothing serious I hope?"

My father shrugged. It meant *who can know* and *what can you expect*. "I might want to go visit her tomorrow," he said.

Dr. S. studied him for a moment. "I think you should go," he said. "But make it brief."

~

The message on the phone at my parents' apartment said the hospital wanted me there right away. My mother had been wandering the halls, disturbing the other patients, even pulling an oxygen mask off one, and they'd had to restrain her.

"Restrain her?" I said, when I got the nurses' station on the phone. "What does that mean?"

"Use restraints," said the nurse on call, who sounded like the tall, dark-haired one.

"Is she restrained right now?" I asked, my voice rising into a rasp. "Is she tied down right now?"

"No-o-o-o," the nurse said. "There's a nurse with her who's trying a redirect. And we've administered a sedative."

I didn't even take off my coat. My father stonily followed me back to the car.

~

When the crowded hospital elevator finally arrived at the fifth floor, I ran down the hall and stopped short at Mother's open door. She was standing by her bed tray on which sat a largely uneaten lunch—a sandwich, a salad, some pie. Her hair stuck out in all directions; she looked like a threatened bird whose ruffled feathers had swelled it to twice its diminutive size. Wetting her finger on her tongue, she was counting out a collection of yellow papers—they looked like the meal request cards. She shuffled them together, patted them down, started again. A slight, soft-faced and very young-looking nurse with a fuzzy blonde perm stood within holding distance of her.

"Mama!" I cried out, gathering her into my arms.

She let me embrace her briefly, her head cocked, then broke away. "Do you hear rain?" she said, walking toward the windows past the now vacated second bed. "The rain is coming in! Don't you see it? Everything is going to get sopping wet."

In a quiet, firm voice, the nurse said. "No, Stella, I don't see the rain. There is no rain." She put her arm around my mother and led her back gently to the bed. Together they sat down. "They're doing a neurological workup," she said quickly to me. "These delusions and hallucinations—it could be something neurological. But it could also be something else. Sometimes being in the hospital itself, especially for the elderly—"

"There is no rain?" my mother asked.

"No, there is no rain."

"But look at the window, it's coming right in!"

"No, Stella, there is no rain."

"I have never, ever seen her like this," I said.

The blonde nurse got up, came over to me. "It's not uncommon," she whispered softly, "my grammy had it before she died. Senile dementia. It comes and goes. You just have to correct them firmly. Sometimes they come back. For a while."

For a few seconds my mother remained on the bed, open-mouthed, staring at the window. But then she leapt up again. She folded her robe, fluffed the pillow on the bed, fussed with the lunch dishes, patted the yellow papers. "It's *very* dirty in here," she said. "I have to straighten up."

Behind us my father stood in the doorway, holding on to the doorframe. "Hello Stella," he said in a flat voice, "How are you doing?"

"Sammy," she said, picking up the pie plate, and brushing away the crumbs underneath, "You should have some blueberry pie. You like blueberry pie."

There was a pause. "I'm not hungry," my father said.

"But you like blueberry pie," my mother said, gathering up the napkins and crushing them together. "This is good blueberry pie."

"Stella, I can't eat. I'm not hungry."

"But you like blueberry pie," my mother said.

"Stella, dear," the nurse said. "He *really* doesn't want any blueberry pie."

"But he *likes* blueberry pie," my mother said, squishing the remains of the sandwich into the salad bowl.

My father said nothing. He stared vacantly, his mouth pressed together.

My mother surveyed the bed tray, hands on her hips. Then she turned to regard the bed. She jerked up the sheet and blanket; a long gauze bandage trailed from under the mattress. She started to shake. The nurse quickly pulled a chair over to the doorway into which my father plummeted, then reached my mother's side at the same time as I reached her. My mother raised one angry fist in the air.

"Mama!" I cried, grasping her tiny frame to my body. She pushed me away on one side and the nurse on the other.

"They accused me!" she said, her arms flailing. "They said I bothered the other patients. But I was only getting some exercise, saying hello to my neighbors, and if I bothered them, I said I was sorry. And then," the tears squeezed out of her eyes, "they tied me down. Four huge women forced me down on the bed and tied me down. It's not *right!* I'm going to call the police. I have my *rights!* They were so *mean.* 'Harder, harder,' one of them said. I couldn't breathe! But I showed them. They won't try that again on me!" she said.

"Mother!" I said, "Oh, Mother!" I tried again to hold her to me. Again she pushed me away with surprising strength. She yelled, "You're just like them, you're acting just like them," recoiling into the arms of the nurse, who grasped her gently but firmly by the elbows.

She jerked free and pulled out another of the gauze bandage restraints she'd stuffed under the mattress. With an expression of nauseated disgust, she held one up, in vindication. "Have you got a scissor?" she said, yanking it as hard as she could, her jaw clenched, "I have to have a scissor."

"I can't take this," my father said under his breath.

"You're here to see this, Sammy," she said. "I'm glad you're here to see this." She still held out the restraint. Then she dropped it, her head dropped, her shoulders shook, and she began to weep silently. The nurse put her arm around her, led her to the bed, and sat her down.

I sent my father home in a taxi.

When I returned, my mother was counting and patting the yellow dinner requests again. The blonde nurse still sat in the room, but it was clear she needed to get on with her other work.

"I have to save these for Daddy," my mother said. "He needs them for taxes."

The nurse got up to leave. "If you need me, ring and I'll come," she said. "See you later, Stella," she said. "Be good."

"What time is check-out time?" my mother said.

"It's a hospital, Mama," I said, "not a hotel."

"Oh, it's a hospital," my mother said. "I forgot." She put down her yellow receipts. "Have you got a dollar," she said. "I'd like to take the girls for coffee."

She got up, went to the bathroom, took a pee. "No shower," she said. "Not a very nice hotel."

"This is a hospital, Mama," I said "not a hotel."

"Oh, it's a hospital," she said, "I forgot. Do you hear singing?"

Hours after all sedatives were supposed to work, she finally fell asleep. I left her after telling the nurses' station that they were to call me if there were any problems and I would come down immediately, and in no case were they to restrain her again.

~

The apartment was, if anything, even neater than it had been before. The bedding on the couch had been put away and the bed still wore its spread. My father looked ashen and frail; he said he couldn't even keep down weak tea. "I don't think I like living alone," he said wanly. Bronchitis or no bronchitis, I took him home with me and put him to bed in the spare room.

~

Saturday morning—rain again. My dog climbed up on one of the kitchen chairs and licked Dad's face. "He thinks he's a mensch," I said, for my dad's benefit. He barely smiled. His half bagel lay on his plate like a life saver he wouldn't reach for. "Maybe you should drink some of that Old-Fashioned Rich Fudge," I said, really worried.

Dad put his hand on his stomach and gave a little nauseated cough just as the phone rang.

It was the diabetes man. "I think we're going to release her today," he said. "The tests were all negative, the drugs for the arrhythmia seem to be doing the job. And, given that she's not a young woman and has a few serious ailments, everything else seems medically okay."

"You're going to release her today?" I said, incredulous.

My father looked up.

No brain cancer, Parkinson's, stroke, organ failure— "Today?"

"Yes."

"They're going to release her today," I said to my father, my heart racing, as I dialed the nurses' station in the diabetes ward to find out when and how. He put his arm around the dog in the chair next to his. He took a sip of tea.

"Two, three hours, tops, probably," said the nurse I got on the phone. I covered the mouthpiece and said to my father, "Two, three hours, tops." He took a tiny bite of bagel. And how was my mother? Well, she was still a little confused, the nurse said, but they had her in this special chair ("the senility chair" used for "redirects"?) and she was manageable. And could I talk to her? Yes, of course.

"Good morning, sweetheart," she said, when she picked up the phone. "I just knew it was you. I tell you, I'm thrilled to get out of here."

"She's thrilled to get out," I said to Dad.

"And boy could I use a good cup of coffee," my mother said.

"Hold on," my father said. "Let me talk to her."

"Stella," he said, "we're coming to get you."

But first, at my suggestion, we put my picnic cooler in the car and drove through the rain to a huge supermarket, the closest we could get to Fairfax Avenue in the sticks. We bought kosher low-fat frankfurters and kosher salami and half-sour pickles, and smoked salmon; we bought salt-free rye and pumpernickel and onion rolls; we bought sugar-free-sort-of-mandel-bread-biscotti, and sugar-free, low-fat, chocolate diabetic ice cream; and on the redolent coffee and tea aisle, we selected a bag of decaf Vienna roast beans for Mom and a package of specialty Orange Pekoe loose leaf tea for Dad.

When Dad entered Mom's hospital room, where she sat, dressed and ready to go, she said "Sammy, dear" and lifted her face to be kissed.

"I missed the rabbi's visit," my mother said, a twinkle in her eye, as we got out of my car in front of their apartment. "He was going to come after Saturday services, but I escaped before he got there."

"Alevai. May it be so," my father said, guiding her by her elbow up the rain-slick walkway, while I, walking on the other side, held an umbrella over her head. "You should take a haircut, Sammy," she said, taking a good look at him, "so long and messy!"

"I'll take a haircut in due time," my father said.

~

So the three of us entered the dollhouse ark. I sat them down on the brocade sofa, put plastic placemats on the coffee table and brought out the feast. We ate with relish—considering the prior knotted and acidic states of our stomachs—the three of us for that moment come smiling from the world's great snare un-caught, victorious against the wanton gods of medical protocol, of illness, and death. Whether my mother's behavior had re-sulted from the arrhythmia, or her own sensory deficits of vision and hearing, or her nervousness in the unfamiliar and fright-ening hospital with its distressing routines, or some combination of these, we would never in fact find out, and we didn't at that moment care.

I brewed my father a cup of strong tea with Sweet'N Low from the "M-O-M" bowl. I ground some beans and served my mother an excellent cup of hot fresh brewed decaf.

"The rain's not coming in from the terrace, is it?" my mother asked, taking a great shluk of her steaming coffee, in the way only she could do. "I'm never sure those French doors are closed all the way."

My father got up to check. "Sealed tight," he said, reclaiming for that brief moment I still love to recall, his guardianship of the nuclear unit we were.

Waiting for News Which Could Be Really Bad

Some days the world's as gloomy
as the window of a medical supplies shop,
where busts and torsos, pelvises and knees—
sporting corsets, braces, trusses—
dustily attest your destined needs.
And in what drab tones. Ochre, buff,
mouse-dun—colors of underwear long stained,
though abstinent—or salmon pink, the therapeutic
color, exactly like the woollies your mother
made you wear. Bed rails, steel canes,
wheelchairs. The body that would rumba, mambo,
tango, cakewalk, clog, jig—reduced
to aided function, too embarrassed
to wear red, even at Christmas.
No bows here,
no lies about gifts.

If you thought suffering was holy—

But all your brief experience of joy,
the work rewarded, the parent brought back smiling
for another test, suggests:
enough blessings and successes
and the old shoe of your heart
bursts its laces, takes in all
the huddled masses

                unless it's grief again

and the heart's gates clamp
like clenched teeth. You hunker down
to pain, familiar as your body's

smells. You live there so long,
you forget your house has other
rooms.

And if some new joy comes, you're thinking,
it will be so unfocusing,
you won't know what to do with yourself
for days.

Death and Belief: The View from Without

My daughter's friend, E., a beautiful, smart, and accomplished nineteen-year-old, was killed in a head-on collision involving a drunk tractor trailer driver as she and a boyfriend drove back to her college town after a rock concert several hundred miles away. It had taken days to locate her, and when her father, leaving her distraught mother in the care of friends, made the four-hour trip, she had been unrecognizable. When I first heard the news from my crying child on the phone, my tears were instant from the shock, the horror. Fast upon that came the heightened sense of a special occasion, of people communing with one another who might not ordinarily. Many people called to find out if we had heard, if our daughter, 500 miles away at school in Northern California, had heard. In moments when I was not busy—making a few calls, for example, to pass on the idea another parent had suggested of establishing a scholarship fund in E.'s name at the high school—I had the abrupt sensation of an abyss opening under me; I imagined my own inability to bear such a grief, pictured falling down, screaming, tearing my hair. At the departing edge of that sensation, came guilt for having the luxury to imagine it, and guilt for imagining that the girl's parents, whatever they might show, whatever they might do that we could perceive, were not living in a nightmare with no hope of waking up.

My husband and I went to the funeral mass at the local Newman Center, although we knew the family only slightly, as other parents active in the high school, parents of a bright student with a future. Our daughter, like E.'s other friends, flew home to attend, leaving the anxieties of the end of freshman year in suspension. Unlike us, she also went to the rosary the night before, and to the cemetery afterwards.

E. was someone I had only a small but real sense of; I knew her mainly through my daughter. The bond I felt most sharply was a bond to the circle of young grievers gathered in her name—each of them beautiful and full of potential, each of their faces unique, pure and stricken. At that time, I had been fortunate enough to have lost almost no people truly dear to me, and no one unseasonably; my parents, after various miraculous escapes, although old, were then both alive and vigorous. I sat at my writing desk after the funeral, in my dark dress, wanting to personally commemorate the loss of E. But all I felt was anger at the cruelty and puniness of life.

~

I realized at that moment that I associated my overwhelming feelings, somewhat defensively and queasily, with my immediate family's lack of religion—whether beliefs, practices or congregation—as if, had I possessed the religious convictions and affiliations most Americans claim, I would somehow have had more "appropriate" emotions. My husband and I thought of ourselves as rootless cosmopolitans—academics and intellectuals—with a self-identification as Jews that was habitually ironic, though I grew up in immigrant New York, the most Jewish city outside Tel Aviv, and he spent his formative years as part of a tiny North Carolina community of practicing Jews surrounded by Southern Baptists. Our identification tended to surface when we read of yet another Skinhead incident somewhere, and had our cynical faith that we would always serve as scapegoats—whether believers or not—reconfirmed. If asked, we professed a kind of loyalty to disbelief, a loyalty that was mostly a negative self-definition by what we were not: members of any community defined by religion, churchgoers of any stamp. I sat at my desk, trying to write something for or about E., but words, saved by no ceremony or etiquette, seemed to me to fall like snow, melting as they fell. They were innumerable as leaves, as bodies, silting up the earth, and the hope that either bodies or words would be pressed and metamorphosed into some new form after some apocalypse of fire seemed immeasurably futile and sad.

~

I went on making calls, talking to those who called, feeling all the while like an ethnographer. In a community of people for the most part affiliated with religious institutions or beliefs of one kind of another who seemed to have dealt frequently enough before with the experience of death to have ready resources, I still felt as if I were acting under false pretenses. It was as if death were a visitor that I alone didn't know how to entertain, though I went along with the motions as best I could. My feelings reminded me of those I'd had at Christmas festivities at college or graduate school; the colors, the tinsel, the carols were American cultural coin, but they still felt strange and awkward, like foreign currency. I had to study them to engage with them, while everyone else didn't think twice.

~

My best friend worried about whether her daughter should be told; she had not been especially close to E. and might get upset and have her school work disrupted. On the other hand, she might also later feel left out if she were not told. My friend seemed to be worrying more about whether or not her daughter was "in the loop" than anything else. Yet I understood her concern; she thought it would be ghoulish to overrespond. I was drawing back, too, feeling, almost, that I had no right to cry, that anyone on the periphery who had a catch in her voice had no right to it. Some acquaintances whose child was also a friend of the dead girl's had catches in their voices that seemed slightly studied when they spoke to us on the phone and I felt uncomfortable, uncertain of the line between feeling and social performance, unsure of how to behave.

I telephoned a couple, favorite teachers of this group of young people, a couple with young children themselves, to pursue the question of putting the scholarship fund into action. They were totally stricken—parents, like us, glimpsing that unimaginable nightmare, and teachers who had embraced this child and sent her out, covered with streamers, flags flying, to impress the world, which took all her fulfillment in one clap of darkness. When youth is taken, we think there is a difference from the full life, the lived life ... as if there really were such a difference ...

~

When my own son was just two and I was filled with the new wonder of parental love, I wrote an essay on Ben Jonson's poem about the death of his seven-year-old son. The essay connected the poem to the Christian and classical literature of consolation for untimely death. But it was impossible for me to imagine—I did not want to imagine—any perspective that could put anything in front of overwhelming love for the unique human child, the love I felt.

> Farewell, thou child of my right hand, and joy;
> My sin was too much hope of thee, loved boy.
> Seven years thou wert lent to me, and I thee pay,
> Exacted by thy fate, on the just day.
> O, could I lose all father now! For why
> Will man lament the state he should envy?
> To have so soon 'scaped world's, and flesh's, rage,
> And, if no other misery, yet age?
> Rest in soft peace, and asked, say here doth lie,
> Ben Jonson, his best piece of poetry,
> For whose sake, henceforth, all his vows be such,
> As what he loves may never like too much.[10]

In the essay, I argued that it was personal unstinting love of the created human child, and not an acceptance of the Creator's will in love for the Creator that led to the concluding vow.

~

The teacher couple, stricken though they were, had galvanized themselves into action, and, one of my ears, listening to them, was tuned to their unfamiliar and alien culture. Mr. T., responding to my mumbling about whether or not my daughter would fly home, took on a strange ministerial tone which I wanted to interpret, at first, as an invasion of my privacy. He told me how important it was for my daughter to come home, to be there, to go to the funeral of her friend; how she would regret it forever if she didn't come. He seemed worried that I had not thought this out. In truth, I had not at that moment even thought that she *might* come; and she had not breathed the idea herself on the phone, having spoken to me before all of her friends began to phone her—and belonging, as she did, to our family, with its peculiar practices or lack of them. Aside from having been fortunate enough not to have *had* to go to many funerals, and to have been exempted from those of a couple of once vivid relatives already misted by geographical and psychic distance when they died, generally I liked to avoid them. I could only recall one funeral, in my immortal childhood (of an in-law aunt rarely seen before), and my children (the son recently graduated from college and the daughter approaching the end of her first year there) had been to none—until E.'s death. Death—still in the category of the universe's personal insult for me—was something I could only imagine being hysterical about or trying to suppress the thought of—in accordance with my upbringing. In my parents' house, funerals were not considered a good experience for children; death was neither talked about nor planned for—an untouchable topic, like sex. Perhaps if it were not thought of or discussed, it would never happen.

~

Mrs. T. urged me to "be strong" in strong tones that came from a source I had no experience of and found vaguely repellent, especially since I didn't feel I had the right to consider being "weak." She was also concerned about another matter. Her husband, an excellent photographer, had been asked by the dead girl's parents to take pictures at the funeral. She was not happy with this idea, seemed to disapprove of it, aside from worrying about how it could be accomplished at all, without embarrassing salience for the photographer. She seemed to be asking a kind of Protestant complicity of me. I wondered if she realized that I was not a Christian; I knew that even if she did, it would be impossible for her to understand the crazy angst I had which I hardly understood myself. Discomfort with my own religion accompanied by a perverse mixture of yearning for and passionate rejection of the religion of the preponderant Other—so compelling, and complacent, as the religion of the Many, and so redolent, for the same reasons, of superstition and treason. This oscillation co-existing with fierce eruptions of the sense that giving up an iota of the cultural identity presumably tied to my own religion would be something like encouraging a treasonous mass suicide.

Misplacedly ethnographic on the phone, I summoned up some irrelevant words about Catholic aesthetics as opposed to Protestant ones. The conversation moved on, by chain of association, to the subject of Mrs. T.'s minister, who had been unable to answer her questions about whether or not people should be permitted to bring photographs of the deceased to funerals. Later, when I described this conversation to my best friend, lapsed Congregationalist and honorary Jewish atheist that she was, she immediately shored me up by expressing my own feeling: why would one expect a minister to help with such questions; answer them for yourself! It was fortunate, I suppose, that my friend's Protestant fear of mental invasion, of having psychological demons supported by a fierce institutional and social structure take up house in one's head, produced some shudders I recognized viscerally—however different their own complex cause. Nevertheless, during dinner at her house the week after the funeral, my friend, as if reading my softening mind on the subject of religion, half-seriously suggested she'd "convert" to Judaism, if I wanted to join the local congregation.

~

My discomfort was perhaps a question of the absence of the tones and nuances of my own natal culture—of its comforting (albeit progressively remote) familiarity. I thought of a program I had watched on TV, a program made by a woman's granddaughter, about her death from cancer. No imitation of Christ, no resurrection, no awaiting the last day and the putting on of a new body. Instead, black humor. Said the mother whose mother had died: "How can I go through the tunnel of death? I get claustrophobia in the Holland Tunnel." But I tended to appreciate Jewish culture largely from a safe distance; if I got too close, *I* got claustrophobia. Maybe it was simply all institutionalized religious or all communal activity—Jewish, Christian, Buddhist, whatever—that I found strange or slightly fearful because growing up in a minority meant *the* community was never really one's own. Maybe I had never gotten close enough to institutionalized Judaism to be comfortable with it. I think I still feared rejection from my own group—for doing things incorrectly, for being an outsider so long—as much as from the others. All the people who belonged to religious institutions in our town seemed to have more in common with each other than I had with them. It had in fact been a Jewish woman whose son had also known E. who'd come up with the good idea of the scholarship fund and gotten it into motion. Mr. T. was not, finally, wrong about the importance of my daughter's coming to her friend's funeral (something she was at that moment in the process of concluding on her own). All of these people, even my own child, felt different from me as I struggled with my para-doxical feelings. But really, all of them were, at bottom, far from unreasonable; they were moved, and kindly, and working off their grief and their fear in ways they thought would cause no pain, and might actually give a little solace.

~

My daughter came home. We hugged, kissed, said some tense words about something trivial, then hugged and kissed again, and discussed the paper she was writing for one of her classes at great length. As if it were a more ordinary occasion, she tried on clothes—first some borrowed from me, then, from a friend—to wear to the rosary, and then, the funeral. She saw an old friend unconnected to E., went with two other old friends to the ro-sary, came home afterwards with them, then had an attack of stomach cramps. I held and soothed her. She wrapped a present for little A., E.'s small brother. I embraced all the girls before they went to E.'s house.

~

I felt so metaphysically alone thinking about religion and eth-nographically observing before we went to the funeral that I had to call my "out of the loop" friend again; she was going to make a contribution to the scholarship fund, but felt too peripheral to go to the ceremony. We had both noticed—it was impossible not to—that the account of E. in the newspaper was hagiographical. It was of a piece with the photograph I would later see on her casket and on the printed program for the ceremony. Slender, beautiful, and blonde, E. had slipped into the role of saint, as if made for it. Her sepia-toned picture, showing her, wraith-like, in a diaphanous dress, gathering flowers in a field, could have been taken in the nineteenth century. She was already ethereal-ized, shrouded by layers and layers of time. The local newspaper confirmed some of what we had heard through my daughter and others: E.'s parents were composed; their faith, their belief in providence, was sustaining them; they were anxious that E.'s friends know that they were welcome, as ever, in E.'s house. I know I felt chilled by the degree to which E.'s parents were apparently able to believe in providence, and that I found some solace between the lines of the conversation I'd had with my apostate friend. My own attitudes to the universe were such that I could only imagine that people put to the test by death, and so cruel a death, would immediately lose whatever faith they had, as opposed to the opposite. Yet, part of me was thinking, what choice does one really have, except to call what happened providence? *Exacted by thy fate, on the just day ...*

~

On the day of the funeral, we arrived at the chapel early; our daughter went to join her friends. My husband and I stood on the sidelines, feeling disrespectful if we were not peripheral, but the teachers, urged us into their embrace. I hugged and kissed Mrs. T. Mr. T. seemed ready to hug too, but I wasn't sure whether to embrace him or take his hands. I did the latter first, then the former. He briefly buried his head on my shoulder.

It's hard to know what to do with one's feelings at funerals. They are social gatherings, and all these people come from such far-off places, and there's fanfare and an air of welcoming. And for us, for me, it was all heightened by the strange gift of our daughter, who had so recently gone off on her own, coming home for an unexpected visit. When we were dressing to go, though our stomachs were in knots and we couldn't eat, I couldn't help but think of "dressing up" when I was a child. My father, his smooth cheek smelling of Old Spice, snapping the paper band off a shirt freshly starched at the Chinese laundry; my mother, talcumed after her bath, attaching her stockings to her garter belt. Then the family, smartly creased and rustling, together and looking good, on the way to the bar mitzvah or wedding.

At funerals, too, the community gathers and people feel bonds to one another, in spite of differences. "It's so good to see you" rings out, though in choked voices. It's as if the deceased is there, at the center, unusually quiet perhaps ... Or maybe it's as if she's there the way a bride is before a wedding, in seclusion, engaged in the mysteries of dressing and anointing herself, and always about to appear. Christianity is already imbued with this image, the image of the faithful one as the Bride of Christ, but I mean it here in a homely and ordinary way. For E.'s parent's, contained, dry-eyed, by whom sat their younger daughter and very small son, for E.'s parents, giving E. the loveliest, the most honoring funeral, wasn't it a little bit like the ordinary wedding she would never have? The chapel, the white and gold, the flowers, the sense of being present at an important passage from one state to another. Until the drapery is taken off the casket, there is an air of expectation, there is a shrouded presence in the church or temple, but it is softened, veiled. And then, suddenly, the harsh under-reality, the wheeled metal frame, emerges, like some sort of alien machinery, and one thinks, again, of a body lying on satin pillows ... and of the earth shoveled on her face.

~

During the mass, to my right, a woman cried intermittently, and told a gold rosary. I had been afraid of this otherness, I realized, most of my life, as if it would find me wanting, show me up, and also, finally make me feel disloyal to my own lineage. Perhaps because I was attracted to its secure dominance, I had studied it through history and literature in a scholarly or intellectual way. I could have given a theological interpretation of the Catholic mass and the bulk of the arguments about its nature that contributed to the Protestant Reformation. Because there were some Jewish people I recognized in the audience, as there had been Christians at the very few bar or bat mitzvahs I had been to at the local Reform temple to which my parents belonged (the boy or girl often inviting friends and parents of friends who were not Jewish), events in both religious houses seemed to blend, momentarily—for someone who belonged to neither. The choir was good, the music appealing, peaceful. I thought about how extraordinary the music written for the Catholic Church has been. The woman telling the rosary looked up at me and smiled through her tears during a moment at which we were asked to clasp hands—the hand clasping was something I'd occasionally experienced at those rare occasions at the local temple.

I tried to imagine what it felt like to be present as a Catholic, what this Catholic ceremony, as such, was doing for the auditors, even to let myself imagine what it could do for me, as I had perhaps done subliminally with all the seventeenth-century Christian poetry I had passionately loved and written about as a scholar. I was struck by the extraordinary focus and thrust of everything said towards the afterlife, towards the theme of resurrection. But, still alien to the core, I was moved, not by resurrection, but by the magnificence of the edifice man had built out of his paralyzing fear of death. And then I began to be chilled by the degree to which the mood was triumphant, by the way in which we were urged to *lose all father* (and mother) *now*, by the way in which the priest's function seemed to be to instill that triumphant mood, and by that aspect of Catholicism that owns and supervises such mysteries of triumph, and owns them so utterly that it can tell you how to feel and what is right. As a kind of myth of solace, shaped by the human community coming together in peace, love, fellowship, I was so ready to accept the providential view urged by the priest, to accept the lack of distinction between a life of one generation and a life of many, to accept the sense that E. "was in a better place." *And if no other misery, yet age.* But, finally, I could only accept such phrasings about E. if I could feel that everyone implicitly understood what they really meant—that is, only that she was "out of any suffering now." Of course there was no such translation, no diminution of the vaulting metaphysics, not even a wink in the air, in a rustle of breeze in that room. But what solace in such a translation? "I believe because it is impossible to believe" Tertullian said. If you do as well as E., the priest said, why stay around? Going from life to eternal life was like going from our mother's wombs where we breathed water to life on earth. One cry and our whole system breathed air. So too, somehow, after our last earthly breath, a new system kicked in and we breathed eternal life. The priest looked up to the ceiling as he performed his function. And clearly he believed absolutely. I began to not only see, but to *feel*, I thought, why the Protestants started Protestantism and rejected priests and prelates for "the priesthood of all believers." It was a rejection of the priest as a higher being, speaking more directly to God than the individuals in the congregation, gathering their prayers and sending them on, mediating for man. But no rustle, not a whisper in the room.

~

Do any of the faithful community see or feel the slippage between the theologies of solace and the contradictory complexities of human feeling? As I, outsider staying outside, see the slippage between some Jewish rituals and liturgy and my feelings that cannot be expressed or contained by them? The woman to my right squeezed my hand kindly when she saw my face. In my head I said what I remembered of the Mourner's Kaddish, known from the few ceremonies I had been to at the synagogue, as well as from the movies, *Yitgadal v'yitkadash* … feeling like a profound faker, though I liked the prayer—an oblique prayer not even mentioning death, exalting eternal God, asking for peace.

What lovely promised peace! Maybe worth the dangers of insularity? Worth overcoming one's disgust at the imperfections, not to mention the pious certainties and intolerances of humans organized into groups? Was anti-religious feeling an adolescent phenomenon? Was I softening, was it time for me to soften? After all, religious feeling is created, contained, defined by the community and certainly I was not truly an outsider, was as much a part of the community, was I not, as the teachers, or the other parents?

Then the greatest and strangest gift—and why to me and not to E.'s parents? My daughter got to fly off again, to take up her life, while their daughter has come home forever. What can I do with this sense of being graced, and no belief in a Giver?

~

It is the end of the summer following E.'s death. My daughter has been home, working hard to help pay for her sophomore year at college. She has put off responding to the urging of E.'s mother, to come visit, to spend some time. She has not forgotten that she promised, so just before going back to school, she goes, and spends three or four hours with E.'s mother. She comes home visibly tense, shaken. E.'s mother has spent the whole time telling her that she must find peace, that she must stop grieving over E. in the way she has, that E. will give her a sign, will let her find peace, if she looks for the sign. E.'s closest friend, a Muslim girl, was given the sign at the end of the traditional period of mourning. And, E.'s mother says, she herself was about to go out of her mind, was unable to eat or sleep, was subsisting on water, until she received a sign from E. and knew she could go on, that it was all right, that this was what E. wanted. It was a light she saw one day, and she knew it was E., and that E. was looking down on her. And after she saw the light, she was able to sleep and to eat. It is providential, it has all worked out. She and her husband had never liked E.'s boyfriend, G., who had been in the car with her, and who escaped fatal injury because he had been asleep, his body relaxed, at the time of the collision that killed E. But now the two families have come to love one another. And indeed, G.'s family tend E.'s grave daily, and heap it with flowers. It is E. who has accomplished this, E. whose spirit has always been the spirit of love. They have no plans to sue the driver who is going to serve too brief a term in prison for manslaughter; they only want him to know something about who E. was, what her gifts were, how much she cared about people spiritually, and they want him to speak of her when he does the community service against drunk driving that is a small part of his sentence.

~

Some months later, my husband and I see someone who looks familiar sitting by us as we wait in a local pharmacy. The man is with a small boy. He looks at us as if he recognizes us and wants to help us out with recognizing him. Finally, we say hello, the context must be making us fail to identify him, ah yes, E.'s father, aren't you? Yes, E.'s father, and how are you? We're fine and you. Oh, we're fine, he says, we're fine, too.

Agnostic Psalm

I praise the Silence for his silent grace
while knives all rest contented in their racks.
I walk on tiptoe past my numbered days.

No midnight phone call bursts my dreams' green haze,
my children safely skip the sidewalk's cracks.
I praise the Silence for his silent grace.

I've no effects, so far, from gamma rays,
my dad's heart has bypassed the speeding facts.
I walk on tiptoe past my numbered days.

Dive for the ground when Gorgon drive-bys gaze,
don't breathe beneath the neon cataract,
and praise the Silence for his silent grace!

Mild kids grin down from freeway overlays,
my love comes smiling from the school of knocks.
I walk on tiptoe past my numbered days.

In valley-of-the-shadow passageways,
no-One's too close for comfort at my back.
I praise the Silence for his silent grace
and walk on tiptoe past my numbered days.

Speaking French

When I speak French on our relatively rare trips to France—a language I studied somewhat desultorily for four years in high school and a year or so in college long ago—the words I am speaking pass before my eyes as if moving across a screen. As I round my lips for the vowels, feel my nose tighten for the nasalization, the words glide by on a schoolgirl's mental moving blackboard, accompanied by their bizarre fantails of mysterious or silent letters reflecting older pronunciations or Latin antecedents—*journAUX, batEAU, fautEUIL*—though I know to say and do say *journO, batO, foetOY*. My husband has never studied the language formally, but has picked up a thimbleful on the street. Of course he hears *J'M, Tu M, Ilz M*, whereas I *see J'aime, tu aimes, ils aiment*; it's as if his French is a kind of pig Latin.

This moving mental blackboard does not disappear when I've grown a bit more accustomed to speaking French. Nor does it produce an annoying sensation. On the contrary, it is more than a pleasant one; it is a constant reaffirmation, a pat-myself-on-the-back, smile-at-the-world pleasure. Just asking for my bread at la boulangerie, buying my wine at la cave au vin, I have managed to cross the gated divide between the letters of French words and their actual pronunciation. I ask the severe and proper madame in her white apron—punctiliously waiting on the pressing crowd in the bakery—for *une à l'ancienne*, just ever so slightly prolonging the final nasal. And she sings back *"une à l'ancienne*-nuh," without blinking an eye, emphasizing her own final syllable just a pinch more (in that way the French have of making even the most mundane conversation into a subtle language lesson). I know I have passed yet another test. And I feel like waving my good grades at the universe. France—the one place my husband and I have attempted to live exclusively in a foreign language—is located in the mouth for me, as much because of these high rewards I garner when I speak, as because of the pleasures of eating its cuisine—including the horns of the warm crisp-on-the-outside soft-on-the-inside loaf of bread *à l'ancienne*-nuh that never made it to the picnic intact.

~

Yet why do I have this memory of a daily glow of accomplishment, a centering focus, even from our fourth trip to France, a brief dash, a couple of years ago? And not from stops in Spain, where I can get along in pidgin Spanish, or even in French-speaking Québec? It probably has something—if not everything—to do with my interiorization of the particular kind of extended stay we had in France, for the nine months of an academic year, in 1993-94. It was a hiatus from our middle-aged lives, an unorthodox sabbatical for my anthropologist husband, a leave of absence from my insecure part-time university teaching job for me, when both of us were sick of the politics of academe and sick of having our egos continually on the line. We were carrying out a plan we'd failed to carry out fifteen years before when our children were little and it had proved too awesomely complicated; it was still complicated (extended stay visa applications for the consulate in L.A. had to be in twelve-plicate, in ink, in perfect French with no cross outs) and got more complicated once we arrived (car registration required the permanent address we didn't have when we bought our used car), but at least we had only ourselves to look out for, no schools to arrange, pediatricians to procure. We did have our laptops (more complications to set *those* up) and our work. But otherwise, we were radically cut off from our multi-tentacled and hugely object-filled American lives—and almost guiltlessly six thousand miles away from my aging parents who had moved to our city almost a decade before—when we finally plunked down in an apartment with few amenities in a little unglitzy beach town on the Côte d'Azur (an oxymoron you may think, but they exist, slightly tarnished and seedy-looking, like beach towns almost anywhere). This one was undistinguished enough to be frequented in the summer only by French folks from further North. And it was a town where no one we knew lived, not even the extraordinarily charming polyglot French anthropologist we met in Paris who encouraged us to go South and helped us find our place (his was about forty minutes away).

Of course, to be suddenly living in exotic French was definitely more dislocating than pleasurable at first. My heavy tongue seemed to flail about in my mouth, like a person who can't find the right position for sleep. And it was difficult to settle in to the idea of actually living and working at my projects in a place whose texture was not in my fingertips, the rhythms of whose weeks were not in my blood and which therefore could give no shape to my life, and yet, whose strangeness at first refused to be backgrounded. Small things distracted me: the light switch that would not fade into inconsequentiality and be flicked on without my thinking as it would have at home, but instead continued to call attention to itself, with its annoying position outside the room the light fixture actually lit, and its peculiar little fuse right there in the switch plate.

That sense of dislocating strangeness, that suspension in time and space is what travelers travel for; it gives permission, on a brief vacation, to not worry about one's usual responsibilities, one's usual self, to imagine change. But I needed ultimately to get on with the academic work I was then deeply into, and to accomplish that I had to be released into the forgetfulness of the familiar and taken for granted. Instead I floundered in a confused time warp. In the morning in the old-fashioned kitchen with its stove and sink on legs, we tried to get the BBC on our shortwave radio, the accent and scene throwing me back into movie—or were they life?—images of the 40s and early 50s. A woman in a checked gingham apron with her hair in big loops behind each ear and puffed bangs over her forehead belonged in that kitchen. Or perhaps what I was feeling as I hunted around for a label for the atmosphere and tried to acclimate myself, was the climate of my dissertation research year in England in the late 60s, when my husband and I, then also without children—our now grown children—were in our twenties.

The fall light, even in the South of France—so ecologically similar to our Southern California with its rocky dry hills and opulent bougainvillea—seemed ratcheted down several notches from the light I was used to, and the wind howled sometimes, echoing in the shafts of our apartment building. The combination of overcast skies and occasionally surprising cold brought me viscerally back to my Eastern U.S. childhood, the fear of cold, the desire for the pleasure of warmth. Indeed the apartment felt grey, gloomy, and full of chill; I was unused to the night-in-day of shuttered windows when I awoke, longing for full flooding sunlight, sunlight to bask in. And, inevitably, French was there every day with its foreignness: a small hill to climb, a detour to manage, a rut in the road to watch out for.

~

After a while, lonely, only able to work for a certain length of time each day, and not always to work well, we gave ourselves over to the new slowness of our lives. We spent long afternoons wheeling our chariot around and around the hypermarché Mammouth, devoid of the technical vocabulary or too embarrassed to try to ask for rubbing alcohol (with the paints, it turns out), or which of the endless varieties of crème fraîche might approximate sour cream, or whether there was any margarine without butter in it. We took slow walks to the post office, a little speech about rates and insurance rehearsing itself in my head if I had a present to mail home. I spent hours planning a phone conversation with a couple who had invited us to call (they'd offered their assistance in the hypermarché), and hours getting up the nerve to actually make the call because, of course, without visible gestures and facial expressions, speaking and being understood in a language you have an uncertain command of is that much harder. I can't say exactly when those slow hours began to glow *because* French was there, and we had begun to accept and even enjoy the inevitable simplification, while occasionally having to wrestle with the complications that resulted from failing to understand so much. And I can't say exactly when that glow heightened *because* French was successfully climbed over, detoured around, managed.

Living in a foreign language is automatically a life-simplifier. It's as if in your own country you are receiving a hundred channels, and suddenly, you are reduced to just a few. You are inside an isolation chamber, like a contestant on a 60s quiz show. Street shouts, conversations in the department store elevator as you ascend, the buzz of TV, can all be easily ignored because they require an act of will to process. Such a life is also disturbing at first because your own cultural identity is shared only with the person you are with; only he or she knows *who you are*. In your isolation chamber, you are an island culture of two surrounded by a sea of French, reliant only on each other for the full range of human interaction spread out at home among other relatives, or friends, or colleagues. Ultimately we grew accustomed to the absence of stimuli, the phone that rarely rang, the lack of e-mail; we began to appreciate the possibility of hearing our own thoughts, even of re-seeing each other.

~

But *living* in France of course requires and invites venturing outside the isolation chamber, approximating being a member of a community. And there, whatever else I was doing—debating between olives with fennel and olives with chili, or admiring the baby of the couple from the hypermarché (who were delighted we'd called and invited us to dinner)—I was also, in measured and tolerable doses, speaking French. And most pleasantly elevated to the stature of number one researcher, informant, and translator for my lavishly competent and knowledgeable—but not in French—husband. Speaking French began to give my days enormous focus and a constant sense of accomplishment, a constant sense of checking off "to-do's" on a list as well as moments of utter annoyance, with my husband loudly whispering in my ear: "What is he saying? What? Tell him he's got it wrong."

It was as if I had one book to focus my days on, one book to hold on to, the book of French, which made me ignore a multitude of other books I might have leafed through, fancied I should read or have read. There was a certain simplicity and completeness, a certain peacefulness in having *one* book. I thought of the ancients who, before the age of material print culture, before the proliferation of books, made an important text truly theirs by memorizing it, and then could endlessly refer to it, find everything they needed in it, locate themselves through it, even use it for divination, be comforted by it.

The words passing before my mind's eye—even the simplest of them, like *thé* for *tea*—with their rakish accents, their smart little hats, had an aura; it went with the pastel curls of ribbon on the white boxes from la pâtisserie, the white frills on the rack of lamb in the butcher shop, the general sense of ceremony that accompanied life, particularly the taking of meals. Everything is aestheticized in France, one could almost say, relentlessly aestheticized, under some kind of penalty to be an aesthetic object—particularly, if not only, women, and the things connected with them. I felt, as I spoke French and was spoken to, as if I were contributing to that decorativeness. Could this have been simply because the French had successfully sold themselves to me as the epitome of cachet, successfully exported a glamorous view of their privileged selves from the time I first pasted a magazine picture of la tour Eiffel on my fourth-grade report cover? And because I was really a snob? This was the European country which, sure enough, had sent the smallest group of immigrants to the U.S. Oh, but it was good that they still pretended they hadn't learned any English, and still tried to legislate against their language going the way of *le weekend* and *le drugstore*, so that I could have the pleasure of eating goose liver *pâté* in a little restaurant with a briefly flashed chalkboard menu, and at the same time could savor the word gliding along my mental blackboard, with its adorable little hat and feather at a jaunty angle, while my husband might well have been thinking *patay*.

~

Of course, in the marriage-cocoon-isolation chamber, I didn't feel the relentlessness of the aestheticization as did the young unattached American computer artist working in Marseille I met at a dinner hosted by the polyglot anthropologist; she was disgusted by the endlessness of naked women in ads for skin cream and chocolate, the endlessness of la maîtresse on the side. As would be my own daughter, a year later, as a student in a very touristy town; she would tell me that the young women she met at parties often seemed *too* careful, afraid to enjoy themselves, to drink enough to get a little high, at a party, for example, for fear of spoiling the *tableaux* they presented. I did notice how a good number of women who seemed to be pushing eighty never let go, still wearing stiletto heels and stockings with clocks, as they clicked down the street in front of our apartment, where dog shit and perfume characteristically assaulted the nose with equal pungency.

But for us, there was, finally, only pleasure in the aestheticization of human interaction in France. Contrary to their press, we found the French almost ineluctably charming, polite, and imbued with a highly developed sense of host-guest relations, though perhaps, at times, we thought, masking some interior sadness. Theirs does seem to be a culture valuing charm over probity. Speaking French made me enjoy being charmed and desire to be charming. And how easy that is when no one really knows *who you are*. I suppose my creditable accent (and not my impoverished vocabulary and limited sense of the finer points of grammar such as the subjunctive) was my charm. Hearing myself in my mind's ear as I rehearsed my speeches with sales people, postal clerks, and ticket agents, or as I spoke and was understood, I almost charmed *myself* with my accent, rather as I attempt to charm myself away from negative self-reflection by smiling at myself in the mirror (a habit my beautiful young daughter found amusingly weird). I did feel some of the friends we made were silently correcting for my errors because they understood enough about the structure of English to grasp the intent behind mistakes English-speakers make when trying to speak French, though not a word of English escaped their lips.. But at least they weren't wincing. My husband even received linguistic compliments when he tried out a few phrases with the sausage-seller at his cart in the hypermarché. Ah, the South! Where, as they themselves say, the people are warmer. (Our landlords, from the North, also said that a friend made in the North was a friend forever, while a Southern friend could smile and smile and forget you immediately. I guess that was their Northern warmth.) If we required incipient Francophilia to get ourselves to France for almost a year, we had it for real, most likely the key ingredient of *our* charm, after a sufficient number of trips to that hypermarché. The cheese counter stretched from here to gastronomic eternity, and each sample was more excruciatingly delicious than the last, and, as we told each other, their lamb tasted more lamb-y, their chicken more chicken-y than anything we'd ever hoped to experience, requiring only tiny portions for full satisfaction that we satisfied our American selves with over and over.

Charm even oozed out of the most modestly employed—teenage servers at McDonald's for example. Could it be that because they were living in the known center of the universe they were spilling over with goodwill and desire to please? "*Monsieur? Madame?*" with the characteristic rising intonation rang out at the beginning and end of every conceivable transaction, even no sale. Even the dentist whose bad root canal and crown cost me a molar came personally to the waiting room to get me, bowed slightly in greeting, saw me to the door after my ordeal, and wished me a good weekend. He maintained his charming politeness until I experienced real distress at the technologically dated impression goo locking my jaws for seven minutes and causing me to gag big time—at which point he got slightly hysterical. But most of the time charm prevailed, and conversations with service people and friends alike, glowing for me with their subtext (*Vraiment, je parle français!*) easily tracked the route of compliment, and didn't stray too far from it, even when cautiously substantive. Perhaps pleasantries are virtually all that is possible in an imperfectly mastered foreign tongue.

~

The charm, as well as the easy accessibility of medical professionals, in particular, was sometimes so palpable, it was actually embarrassing for one more accustomed to routine brusqueness. I had some troubling symptoms in France which resulted in a gynecological exam and, later, an ultrasound of my uterus. The gynecologist performed the ultrasound himself in his office; doctors, greeted as *Monsieur* or *Madame* and not *Docteur*—just as they greeted their patients—seemed to be far less august and priestly figures in France and had few technicians to do auxiliary work for them. This one was remarkably handsome, which didn't help at all. As he moved the ultrasound wand across my plumpish belly, I was suddenly taken by acute apologetics for my excessive flesh in the land of the genetically thin and blurted out something about "*un peu grosse.*" "*Mais non,*" exclaimed Monsieur M., "*Pas du tout!*" and then something like "*C'est necessaire …*" or "*Il faut avoir… ,*" seeming to cross the doctor and courtier or suitor wires, causing me to lose the remainder of his sentence and, blushing hotly, crawl inside my head in a paroxysm of embarrassment.

~

Were our increasing experiences of delight (even the gynecologist was cherishable, of course) simply the mirrors of the Francophilia we increasingly projected, as we grew more in love with this savory and fragrant hiatus—contained in new accents—from our everyday lives and tensions, becoming more and more accustomed to once strange textures and rhythms as our remaining weeks diminished? Where could one find someone so *aimable* as the man behind the counter even at the little local market across the street, who with graciousness, and indeed a kind of measured enjoyment, was always willing to give a little disquisition on the flavors and best accompaniments of his relatively small selection of cheeses? Of course, I usually began by saying how much I loved all the ones he'd sold me before. And we were, unlike my student daughter, the only Americans in town. Where could one find such delightful friends as the French family we fell into a kind of dinner and outing schedule with, and invited to meet our American friends when they passed through, and with whom we exchanged such charming hostess gifts, such sincerely-meant oh-you-really-shouldn't-have's? But would we have so enjoyed these acquaintances, would we have made these same friends if they didn't speak French? For me, speaking French was a little like an infusion of youth, a reminder of that time when—confident of beauty, sure of the spotlight—one lived and at the same time glamorously watched one's self living, as if on a stage.

When we returned to France—this time to Normandy which we'd never seen—for a brief week and some days four years after living there, I had to take the language out of mothballs, air it out, try it on again. After a day or two, after a few tastes of bread and cheese that reawakened taste buds I thought were forever dead, after a pleasant conversation with an hôtelier originally from the South, I began to find that place in my mouth and mind again, the pleasure of knowing the few subtleties I know: *baguette*-tuh! *fromage*-zha! But our visits are inevitably few and far apart, and I am not a polyglot, so when I go again, I will undoubtedly be blissfully unable to forget, that I am speaking French.

Charm

Is it possible to charm
the spouse who's heard you
fart in bed? The child
you've screamed at?
Isn't charm only a long white glove
removed, fingers extended,
charmed, I'm sure
kind of thing?

And didn't Jeffrey Dahmer
have it? And Ted Bundy?

My freshman year boyfriend—
the slick dancer
from a lovely New England
home, back in the double-standard
60s—almost charmed the pants
off my prim mother, and,
I learned later, had been engaged
in the gang rape of a townie girl.

It's enough to make you put on
tiger skins and seek the desert.

Yet, sometimes I cannot feel
my face until I put on
my smiling interaction mask.
Alone, in my blue room,
stewing in my own
juices, I begin to
dissolve, then evaporate.
I need the press of others

to make me condense,
though my attempt
at charm, fashioned
to interface, can feel like
an invader surrounded
by leukocytes—utterly
resisted.

Still, talking on the phone
this morning, asking a favor
of a friend, I felt my cheeks
chunk up with goodwill,
and my internal organs
all peacefully nestle.
This afternoon, even my dog
put on the dog of good behavior—
heeling properly, as if
trained   when my visiting grandson
held his leash for his walk.
And as I apply my lip gloss
and blush this evening
before going out, bizarrely I smile
at myself, trying to disarm
my deep doubt—charmer
and charmed at once.

Bless us all—social beasts
that we are. We dish up
smiles, we laugh in self-deprecation
as we flick cookie crumbs
from our lips, we try to lift
our blue-footed booby feet
in sync with a potential mate's,

to lubricate the wheels
of social traffic with our luscious
dimples—as if we could soften
the world and shape it
to our needs—our moon faces beaming
on our compatriots, dark sides
sweetly hidden.

Resident Dead

I glimpse over the cemetery's stone wall the Hallmark seasonal window effect, as I slow, driving on a less-than-everyday route in my dusty Western town: Halloween pumpkins, paper and real, all over the grass, a large scarecrow of raffia and printed cloth near one grave. I have visited my mother's grave in the small, largely unadorned Jewish section just once since she was buried there years ago on a hot July day. I cannot imagine bringing plastic bouquets, mylar balloons, butterfly pinwheels, porcelain lambs and angels like those I remember decorated most of the flat stones, or even a small July 4th flag like the few that waved over the Jewish dead—housewarming presents for the name-plated doors of death's local habitations. Yet now my mother's wizened corpse in her coffin floats over the graves into my mind. The skin is taut on her bones, brown and papery as the skin of mummies, the mouth drawn back, the few teeth exposed ...

But is skin left? Pleistocene slowness or puffball speed?—I have no idea of the time to dissolution. Could she still be dressed as I instructed for the closed coffin service—neither in the customary white shroud, nor as if she were going out to meet her Maker in good viewing style: suit, jewelry, pumps—but as if we two were cheating the Angel and she were going in for a long hospital stay? The old velour robe, the hospital booties, the floral nightgown—already dust, or mildewed into juice? Dust the chipped pink polish on the nail of her dangling little finger, which I stroked that last night? Dust the fleshed finger? Yet "my mother is buried in Olivewood Cemetery," a *place* to stop, or not. Had she been whisked from my last glimpse of her on her hospital bed, her ashes scattered to the atmosphere, to whirl with rocks, and stones, and trees, would I like my dead nonresident?

Or would I have felt a restless permanent unease, like hers—as she wanders through eternity—as some rabbis warn? I read somewhere the Romans cut off a little finger for burial—did they hope to ground the spirit?—before they burned the body.

I clasp that last glimpse, the whole body dressed for a night's sleep, before it slides under the lid of earth, because it seems easier for the resurrection I don't believe in to occur with the rudiments of bones and hair and teeth in the neat package of the coffin—an erector set in disassembly, an eternal life kit—than with dispersed dust lifted and sunk on the winds, spirited into the heavens and falling again in the rain. As if reassembly were an imaginable task for an only semi-great God-I-don't-believe-in: a jigsaw puzzle after tea in the retirement home rather than the mystery of the first carbon molecule, Jehovah bending close to breathe on some random handfuls of dust—a plume of which I leave behind, the convened atoms of my body accelerating, bound, right now, where I aim.

Useless Knowledge

I am a repository of information
that won't die. I know
precisely, for example, what my mother
liked to eat, though to know is like
keeping instruction manuals
for appliances long ago
sold or donated to Goodwill.
I could check off her
hospital menus for an eternity,
if necessary, order for her in
the restaurants of heaven. She liked
rye toast "well-done,"
the unfertilized eggs
inside freshly killed chickens
(but she gave them to me). She loved the feet
of those chickens, noodles
and cheese—even
that same cottage cheese gone off
(*farshtunkene kez!*)
and scrambled with eggs,
and, as at the Denny's,
a few days before she died,
the very rare sundae,
hot fudge, with "burnt almonds."
The longing came over her,
my tiny mother, and she glinted
the glint in her eye,
saying Dr. B. told her
she wasn't "really a diabetic
anymore." But we shook

a stern finger, and muttered
about control, and now I am left
with this blank before
her still unordered
"last good meal."

Woosh!

I am on my way to take Dad to the urologist. He has prostate cancer, which he has, of course, forgotten. It is a hot June morning in Southern California, after days of marine fog. The jacaranda trees are strewing purple petals like wedding guests showering brides and grooms.

When I get to the assisted living residence he is not sitting in the chair where someone usually deposits him—after I've called several times to remind them to remind him to be ready, which, of course, he forgets, as soon as he is reminded. I check the other building where he sometimes goes on his better days in search of "some action"—Bingo, or the occasional entertainer. Nope. A staff person emerges—oops, he must have gotten on the bus taking residents to the drugstore. The executive director calls the bus driver by radio. I drive back up to the drugstore (where I have just been to buy the denture tablets he forgets to use) and find him sitting in the facility van. The bus driver hands him over to me.

"We have a doctor's appointment," I say.

"Woosh," he says—his now most characteristic sound—a quick expulsion of breath through loose, slightly everted lips, a kind of strong sigh. "I didn't know."

He is not entirely steady on his feet, as if he's forgotten for a second what walking is, or maybe he's forgotten where he is, or didn't recognize it in the first place—this little shopping center a half-mile from where he lives now. He's wearing the same light-colored jeans—pee-stained around the fly—that he was wearing a few days ago when my husband and I took him to dinner, and a few days before that, when I dropped by to give him a new darker blue pair I'd bought.

"Woosh," he says, getting himself into the car awkwardly, feet all a-fumble.

"We're going to the doctor," I say.

"Oh. Any particular reason?" he asks.

I explain, roughly, about the prostate cancer.

"Oh, I didn't know," he says.

~

I turn off the radio that comes on as soon as the car starts. I present the positive side. He'll just get a manual exam and a hormone shot. To control the prostate problem he has. I don't discuss the radiation treatment possibly on the horizon—every day for eight weeks. When the radiation oncologist found out my father was 87, he said no, no need for *that*, clearly doing a quick statistical computation. Chances of dying before the cancer kills him? Something or other percent. On the other hand, the urologist—who has actually looked in my dad's face during three appointments, and who knows he's otherwise healthy—has talked of the optimum treatment as hormone therapy *and* radiation. Though last time he did say hormone therapy alone was a "good choice we have made together"—and I tried to decipher what that was code for.

Now, as we whiz down the boulevard under the blithe opulence of the jacarandas, I try to engage my father's long-term memory. I take his left hand in my right; his signature strong squeeze isn't quite forthcoming. What I want to know is how exactly he left Germany in 1934. I know his eldest brother, now long dead—who ran away from home as a kid, stowed away on a ship, and wound up in the U.S.—was the one who arranged visas for my grandparents, and for my aunt and uncles (now mostly gone or ancient and sick). But it occurred to me this week that I don't know what the difficulties for a Jew—even a Jew with a visa—leaving the year after Hitler came to power might have been. I don't even know what port he left from. But I wind up feeding him more information than he gives me.

"I think I flew," he says.

"In 1934?"

"It must have been a ship, then," my father says. "My brother would know. Woosh."

I have to take my hand back; we stop for a long red light.

"And how is Duhvid," my father says—maybe for the fifth time since I took him off the senior van—sweetening my husband's name, as he always does.

"David's okay," I say.

"And how are the children," my father says, also for the fourth or fifth time. I can feel his brain grinding through its gears. "How is Danny," he says. For a second I imagine my father imagining the children—actually flung world-wide—in their beds at home.

"He's fine. He's still in Latvia," I say. My son is doing research for his PhD in Riga—at least some of the time—while trying to nurture a long-distance relationship with his girlfriend, who is researching hers in St. Petersburg, Russia.

"Oh, that's right, he's in Latvia." The name comes off his lips with the aural equivalent of a vacant stare. The gears grind again, this time, more protractedly. "And how is Mara," he asks. "She's fine, right"?

"She's still in Morocco," I say.

"That's right. She's in Morocco," Dad says.

My daughter, in fact, called this morning. Her language course is over, and she's packing for her return to the U.S., anxious about the job hunt to come.

It's June, that time of year that marks the passage of time for me—school, including the university where I teach, moving to a close, graduations in the air, eternal summer beckoning, and I wish I could shower both of my children with success and happiness as lightly and easily as the jacaranda strews brilliant purple.

"But, they're both happy," he says. "I mean, they're *happy*."

"They're okay," I say.

"Woosh," my father says. And then, as we enter the parking lot of the medical building, "Oh, we're going to the doctor."

"Yes," I say.

"Any particular reason?" my father says.

~

Dad opens the door and shows me in to the urologist's office, as if he were a very well-behaved suitor on a date. There is no one in the waiting room, and at first, I am afraid they have scheduled him with the male nurse alone on a day when the doctor is in surgery, which would be a problem, since I really need the doctor to do that digital exam, and to tell me that we can continue to make that "good choice" of hormone therapy "together," at least for now. I am thinking, selfishly, of how much I want to get away for a couple of weeks this summer, and of how that will be impossible if David—even sweetened David— and I have to alternate taking Dad to radiation therapy every single weekday. Which, in spite of the assurances about how well it is tolerated—on the part of the doctor, who hasn't experienced it—sounds nasty. Partially in recompense for my thoughts, I reach across the chair arms to give my dad's liver-spotted, thick hand a squeeze. I stroke the left side of his also spotted bald head, his coarse fringe of white hair. I smile at him crookedly. And he smiles back with that good-natured, self-effacing grin, as if we have just shared a mild joke at his expense. That reflex immigrant ingratiation, even with his American-born daughter? Or his intrinsic sweetness of nature? I still don't know. I give him one of the numerous magazines I have brought along. He studies the cover carefully. Then he scrutinizes an ad on the flip side.

"And how are the children?" he asks.

I repeat what I've already said, adding a bowdlerized version of Mara's job anxieties. What the hell.

"She's always had a good head on her shoulders," my father says. "She knows what to do. Right?" He still has the surgically implanted rose-colored glasses of his immigrant generation.

Is this purely phatic here-we-go-round-the-mulberry-bush conversation really that different from all my conversations with my father, convinced always that his American child, and—if anything, even more—his American grandchildren must possess all the ingredients for sterling success and exemplary personal happiness? Now I'm not sure *I* remember if he's *always* been like this. How long will my own memories last before they go woosh? Oh, but I do remember *this*: the optimism transfused in his twenty-one gun "smile and the world smiles with you" treatment, applied intensively, hands on, when either grandchild felt low. Odd thing is, it was pretty effective.

I wish my father could smile my son into calling him more often, even if their conversation dims more than it brightens—like a lamp with a bad connection.

~

Four years from now, my son will have married his smart, kind and cute girlfriend, and will be finishing a stint at a U.S. Embassy overseas on Valentine's Day, when he has a "pure grandpa moment." He will impulsively duck into a supermarket and buy boxes of chocolate for everyone—the cooks, the drivers, his co-workers—and then go back and get a second box for the drivers, because there are so many of them.

~

"Well, when you write to the children, give them my very best," my father says, putting my magazine down with the pile on the waiting room table. I gently retrieve it.

~

Four years from now an East Coast cousin will call me up and tell me she *must* move closer to her grandchildren. She has just had dinner with service-oriented Mara, who now works—for a nonprofit with global harmony goals—in the same city where my cousin's grandchildren live; my cousin says she *covets* the role Mara's grandfather had in her life. "'He was the person with the single greatest influence,' your daughter said! I *want* that!"

The author's father with her daughter at a family event in Arizona. 2000.

~

But now it is June, 2001, and we are waiting in the doctor's examining room; Dad's in the one chair, I'm on an extra stool. I have told the male nurse who ushered us in that we are hoping we can still put off radiation, if the doctor thinks the signs are good. He leaves and comes back with Dad's hormone shot, making a joke about schoolgirls sent out into the hall as he sends me out into it. "So, you want to go on radiation," he says confusingly, when he opens the door again to let me in. "No," I shake my head. "We want to put it *off*." "I didn't understand a word," Dad says, buckling his belt, as the nurse exits. But he seems to intuit there's exasperated air in my lungs. He gives me that little self-effacing grin, as he sits down again in the one chair. He has shaved erratically; there are long hairs under his chin, and some on his upper cheeks. "I feel as if I have one more baby," I say, to him, wiggling his nose.

But I want to travel this summer, many summers, while I still can, I am thinking. I want to host gala June weddings for my happy children, when they marry smart, kind, and cute significant others. I want my father, his hair black, to grip the children's hands and mine in his vise-like paw, saying, "See, what did I tell you! They have good heads on their shoulders." I want him to be uncommonly gracious to my long dead mother as they kvel over the grandchildren's mazel.

"I hope I don't act like a baby," my father says, turning up the smile wattage. I stroke his bald head, which feels as much mine as a clay pot I am shaping on a wheel.

~

The doctor arrives. He shakes my father's hand warmly; my father, who has just asked me again what office we are in and who we are seeing, nevertheless looks at him as if he were a long-lost landsman, or the brilliant nephew recommended by a best friend. The doctor immediately launches into that well-meaning but tortured mode of speech which is, I think, a measure of his difficulty saying what is scientifically accurate in language that might have a chance of communicating to ordinary mortals. I glean that my father's bloodwork is good. I step out again while he does the digital exam.

When I come back, the doctor and I talk about fingers and how accurate they are, while my father, buckling his belt, continues to beam beatifically. The phatic vibes are excellent. Reprieve, once again reprieve! From whatever it was that lurked in the jaws of the future. I mumble about "quality of life ... difficult decisions." The doctor goes on about the sound choice we have arrived at together, at least for the moment, and how we'll reevaluate in four months when we may well encounter a decision fork. Or, possibly, not.

A phone rings in the examining room. "I'm not here," my father says gaily.

In the elevator on the way down, his arm in mine, I mumble about long-term decisions. "I'm not complaining," my father says. "I'm an old man. But I'm not complaining."

We step out into the dazzling sun.

"I mean as long as you're helping me ..."

"No point in talking now then?" I say, pressing his arm a little tighter against me, as we negotiate the steps.

"Exactly," he says, righting himself from a slight falter as he transitions to flat ground.

Together our eyes scour the parking lot; I spot the car that used to be his and we set off towards it.

"And how are the children?" my father says.

Woosh.

Yiddish Kisses

And another one (as if
the first): reverently, on my hand—
papa the courtier—your walrus
moustache splotchily wet. And
an encore: you miss
my hand in your hand and
kiss your own.

At your luncheon table
in the dementia wing, you've clasped
both my hands like prayer
times two above the soup.
Looks like broccoli-cheese, something
inedible. On our right,
a glowering resident twists away
from the looming spoon. Again you touch

my hand to your lips, then deposit
another wet word juicily
on my cheek—not quite missing
my ear—as if to speak
my nickname, *katchkele*. The papery
dowager on our left tremors down
her spoon and stares: envy? desire?
disgust?

I force-feed you smiles and you
smile back, electric,
and kiss me on the forehead,
pinning there a blue
ribbon for some virtue I've

hardly shown—staying but
planning escape.

I stroke your dry, bald head.
It's almost as if
you've grown fur, like the ancient
dog at home—out of his own small
skull, arthritic, shambling
along, stumbling, dropping his
back end, barking *let me in!*
barking *let me out!*

I almost wish you were furred.
So easy, so soothing for me,
to stroke your head again.

Shame

My father's eyes stayed closed. Standing behind him, as he lay in his narrow bed, I stroked his warm, almost hairless scalp. The hospice doctor, finishing the examination for which he'd come, poked my father's feet with a pin. No reaction. My father's cough gurgled, thick. The hospice nurse leaned in and deftly snuck a suction tube into his throat; he gagged, arms flailing, writhed away from her. Then, abruptly, he quieted, his breath still ragged. I took up my post again, smoothing the sparse white strands at the sides of his head. When I was little, my father let his giggly only child fluff out his then-thick hair. It was our *Herr Doktor Einstein* game. It didn't bother him to look ridiculous. Now—the overseer of his care and sometime caretaker—I had access to his body again; I cleaned his crusty nails with a metal file from my purse, held a tissue around his nostrils for him to blow into when I visited the facility, where nothing was easy—even before my father started dying.

"You must love your father very much," the pinstripe-suited doctor said. He sat, one leg over the other, on the old leather recliner I had brought from home for my father's room. He propped his clipboard and paperwork on his knee.

It was a long time before my father took another noisy breath. I looked down; his blind hand sought his belly and rested there, just under the sheet.

"He must have been a very good father," the doctor said, scribbling away.

"He was," I said. My immigrant father, with faintly Germanic attitudes about the body. The swimmer who taught me to swim, while my mother fearfully splashed herself at the edge of the sea. The opener of his overcoat on frigid winter walks from the subway. "It's not *really* that cold. Breathe in. *Ahhh.* Breathe out."

The man who took me into the shower with him when I was four and five, whose genitals were the first adult male ones I saw—unthreatening, matter-of-fact—who made the point that there was nothing to be ashamed of in our nakedness, in any part of us. The one who sat near me when, at thirteen, I writhed on the couch with menstrual cramps, who told me stories of sisters and old girlfriends who survived them. The man who signed the secret permission letter that allowed me to be fitted for a diaphragm at the Margaret Sanger Clinic, when, at 19, I wanted to sleep with my fiancé ("You are sure, right? And he is committed to you?")—a letter my mother would have considered shameful, especially if anyone knew.

I stroked his forehead and scalp, my fingers trying to speak. My father inched his hand further, just inside the diaper the sheet barely covered, and rested it on his penis.

"I mean I've rarely seen your degree of devotion," the doctor said, still writing.

I reached down, quickly lifted my father's hand by the wrist, and moved it away.

Sudden as my mother's judgmental eyes, a bizarre impulse of propriety? Because his death was on a public stage? The audience, strangers? My father gave me a gift, which I thought I'd kept. But I censored him, taking away a little flame of comfort he might still have felt. And was ashamed of my shame.

"You really are a good daughter," the doctor said, looking up, smiling.

In the Doctor's Office, Two Weeks before His Death

What was my father dreaming,
hunched in his wheelchair,
zipped neck-high in too warm fleece,
tired eyelids gently closed,
fingers meekly interlaced
in soggy lap?

Even his waking
was a kind of dreaming. As if he had become
a dream self that he watched—a self so
patient and he unable
to shake him, so silent,
and he unable to make him speak.

And he waited—always in
the moment's blink—without knowing
he was waiting, as now
he waited to be summoned
by the doctor's nurse, to glide
to the examining room (myself
anonymous behind), the rain
of stimuli erased as if by
windshield wipers, then again erased,
again, again, again.

His brain was ratcheting
crazily backwards until it spun
blindly off its sprockets; it was
a print left too long in the developer
until it became all blackness.

But suddenly he smiled with such
sunburst graciousness—what *was*
he dreaming?—and murmured so
distinctly in his sleep, "That looks
so *nice!*" as if his soul leapt
to an instant of shining reassembly,
like broken glass in a film run
in reverse.

Brief Dip into Ethnicity

I have not worn a Star of David around my neck since my childhood in the Bronx, having long felt that peculiarly minority feeling that to assert one's identity is to be divisive—though the majority can blithely wear the symbol of a Christian nation. I have also felt that my own ethnic group might be the first to point out that the star symbolizes more than mere ethnic identification—that is, some sort of commitment to practice, study, knowledge. By such measures, my own Jewishness is highly diluted, weak as a fifth cup of tea brewed with the same teabag.

Even in my Bronx childhood, my sense of Jewish identity wafted in at a merely nostalgic remove; since my bedroom overlooked the Orthodox synagogue next door to our building, the haunting music of the liturgy, the recitative of prayer, was often in the foreground of the city's white noise. But we were not members of the congregation. My mother, who spent her girlhood in Lemberg and Vienna, did keep a number of domestic Jewish rituals and holidays, but gradually lost all but Passover in the course of her long American life, even if she never lost her fiercely Jewish and pro-Israel sense of self. When my parents retired to my California town, they did join the local Reform temple at my suggestion—which did turn out to be a good conduit to a social life. My father seemed to grow vaguely fond, then, in his retirement leisure, of the rituals that reminded him of the religious customs of his Orthodox family when he was a child in Duisburg, Germany. He became "famous," by all accounts, in that temple, emceeing Thursday night Bingo with enthusiasm and a little highly successful rude humor, running the temple gift shop with business and artistic acumen and *poysonality*. But he was no believer—as he'd told me from the time I was little—and anything but officious about the whole institution. He loved to joke in private about the temple yentas and big shots, and the "hullabaloo" about one thing or another at committee meetings.

With their German-Yiddish accents, overlaid by a Bronx brogue—my parents were *the* purveyors of Yiddishkeit to goyim, apostates, and weak Jews alike, by order of history. As long as they were around, whatever cultural Jewishness I felt was inevitably externalized in them. As for myself—well, I was a citizen of the world, set far apart from my more chauvinistic relatives, including my mother. My suburban California children were raised without any formal religious training at all, even if my daughter, the younger child, picked up a little atmosphere when grandpa and grandma occasionally took her to Sabbath or New Year services at the temple. My children did deeply absorb their much-loved grandfather's story, of how he was visa'd away from Nazi Germany in 1934 along with a younger brother, a year after his parents and their youngest child immigrated to New York—all through the auspices of that older brother who had rebelled at an early age, stowed away on a ship, made it through South America into North America, and into a successful New York businessman's life with good "connections." They deeply absorbed the fact that my father's eldest sister and her husband, feeling too established to leave with their young children, remained in Germany, and were killed—though my father rarely spoke about his eldest sister and her family and how they died, and did not know exactly where. Still, my children's sense of Jewish identity—undoubtedly as a result of the choices I made for them, as well, perhaps, as the multiculturalism of their educations—is rather theoretical and abstract, owned up to as a matter of principle, when they encounter a whiff of anti-Semitism in some foreign experience in their well-traveled lives, but unconnected to practices, education, or even much in the way of memories, and that much more removed from my own more and more remote culturally Jewish childhood in New York City. In short, their identities as Jews seem in no way *visceral*.

When my mother died, my father no longer made the long drive to L.A.'s Fairfax Avenue, for kosher meat, as well as zaftig starches and cholesterol khazerai—challah with raisins, desert-plate-size "black and white" cookies, hamantaschen, rugelach, marble cake, crumb cake, babka—all of which used to be offered to us, or were part of the frequent dinners my family and I enjoyed at their apartment. My father managed for a number of years, then slipped more and more into the haze of Alzheimer's and was finally persuaded to move to a "retirement home." The one close enough for my frequent visits had strong Christian nuances. My weak identity had grown that much weaker; Jewishness occupied virtually none of my mental space. Every once in a while, a temple friend of my father's—convinced he would be enheartened by it—arranged a brief Sabbath service for the two or three Jewish residents and the others who trailed along in an Alzheimer's fog (just as my social father followed his co-residents into their Sunday Bible Study group on several occasions) and I got wind of it, and was urged to come. To my amazement, my father, who spoke little now, could still hoarsely chant the brokhe over the bread and wine. I stood there, feeling mainly a short-lived embarrassment about my lack of Hebrew.

And yet, and yet ... of course it wasn't really some china *cup* into which I dunked my weakening Judaic tea bag; I knew, of course, it had to be a *glass*, a *glezele tey*, and the tea had to be sucked up through a sugar cube held in the teeth. And I was enough of a Jew to shudder slightly, without thinking, whenever a group of Hasids passed by, in their white shirts, fur hats, black coats—their glossy peyes jouncing under their spectacle ear pieces, gorgeous as little Dorothy's ringlets in *The Wizard of Oz*—just as my mother—for all her visceral identification with her people—always did. Some Jews were "bad for the Jews."

~

What a watered down ethnic identity! Once in a while I felt guilty about it, for having "broken the chain." I felt guilty for being bound to "my" people—like other Jewish nonbelievers—by an identity with no active content, only the terrible negative of the Holocaust. Yet that identity *could* suddenly take me by the throat.

On a trip to Berlin for his job, my son visited the Jewish Museum on a whim and discovered a book about the Jews of Duisburg which listed every member of my father's family, including the rarely mentioned eldest sister; my son photographed and emailed the pages. It was viscerally shocking to see those few names I had never heard, along with my would-have-been aunt Paula's, starkly linked to the dreaded place of their deaths. Paula's husband, Mendel, their young daughter Charlotte, and little son Hermann are all described as dead or "lost track of" in Auschwitz, Paula having unsuccessfully applied in 1938 to join her family in New York.[11] My father's deliverance and my own consequent existence seemed almost magical, in contrast. But my father was already much too confused to absorb such information, and too fragile to deal with it were he able to absorb it. Unshared with the person to whom it most belonged, it seemed to pass into some cloudy otherwhere after the initial impact.

Then my father died, at ninety-two, five years into his Alzheimer's, and, as his only child, thrust into arranging his funeral, and into a sharp awareness of my minority status in my suburban California town, I became—almost—viscerally Jewish again. And I realized—even if I would never wear the star—how important it had been and was that my parents wore it *for me*, even in their deaths.

~

In accordance with the Jewish custom of rapid burial, I had immediate arrangements to make, just as when my mother died, ten years earlier. My daughter—the first of my two children to arrive from the East—came with me to the funeral home. Mr. H., the agent, apologized for being a little unsure of himself; it was only his second Jewish funeral (and my third). No open casket? No embalming? No visitation? No *flowers?!* We chose the coffin from the few Jewish pages in the catalogue; it appeared to have a simple wooden Star of David, like the one my mother's coffin had. Mr. H. went to the window with us, peering closely at the picture. "I think there's a star. Yes, definitely, there *is* a star." The star was placed just over where a knight's shield would be, I remember thinking; I had made rubbings of memorial brasses while researching my doctoral dissertation in England. I mentally hit myself on my forehead with the flat of my palm. *Mogen David!* Shield of David! Then I made a further mental note to check out the possibly irrelevant assumptions I had just leapt to. For all my father's complexity, it was hard to imagine burying him any other way. The star felt like part of his familiarity—friendly, a guide, even a password I had to be sure he had for his final trip.

At the temple the next day, I was guiltily grateful for the air of quiet sanctity that made this day different from all others, an air untarnished by habit. I was glad, but felt undeserving, to be greeted in so kindly a way by the people who had loved or liked my father—though only a trickle compared to the capacity turnout at my mother's funeral, when my parents were the temple's old-world icons, and he had not yet begun to drive the wrong way up one-way streets. I partook of the nonbeliever's, non-temple-goer's guilty pleasure of identification with her "own." These people acted as if we were each one of theirs, though we would probably never see them again.

~

Just a few minutes before our family sat down in the sanctuary, the rabbi I'd just met in person called me into his study and went through some instructions about the funeral, but was mostly busy on the phone, attending to other matters. Most of his energy had gone into correcting me when I'd asked "How are you?" and shook his hand.

"We don't ask 'How are you,'" he said. "How can a person *be* on the day of a funeral?"

"Sad," I said, ever the good student.

"Aha!," he said, his index finger in the air.

While in the study, I'd decided I'd better give him the customary gratuity I'd been instructed about by temple-going friends of my dad's. The rabbi gleefully snatched the envelope containing the check out of my hand, like a comedian. "I can do this!" he exulted, "I'm leaving in June!" I had opened the box of religion. But I would choose only what I fancied; I could put something back after taking a bite, too.

Soon after I had rejoined my family in the sanctuary, the rabbi emerged from his study to greet us. He put his prayer books on one end of the lustrous, dark wood casket, about where that knight's shield would lie beneath the lid, so he could give each of us a little black mourner's ribbon to pin to our dresses or lapels. He tore mine first to symbolize the Biblical "rent garments" I knew about from some literary context or other and handed it to me. He seemed a little uncomfortable with my husband, who was wearing a fedora and not a yarmulke. They had previously briefly conversed when the rabbi had telephoned to discuss the funeral and gravesite plans. My husband said something about "celebrating a life" before passing the phone to me. The rabbi told him: "Jews don't celebrate at funerals." Except for his moment of slapstick comic relief, he was consistent, I guess.

I could sense my son standing stoically with his wife, on the other side of my daughter, accepting the ribbon, but making himself psychologically absent—his feelings unconnected to these ministrations. I needed to have my father at my side, respectful for the moment, so as not to cast any aspersions, but squeezing my hand in a way that meant *What a shmegegge! We'll laugh our hearts out in the car on the way home.* My daughter was tugging my left hand and whispering in my ear: "I don't see the star! Do you think it could possibly be under the books!" The rabbi tore and gave the last ribbon to my daughter. Her cheeks, like mine, were wet.

My children and I read three very personal eulogies celebrating my father's love and tolerance—in spite of, or because of his past—and his generosity and gentleness. The rabbi perked up, complimenting each eulogy as better than the last, then read a cheesy poem. But before all of this, the rabbi had lifted the prayer books off the casket, and ascended the steps of the bimah. And my daughter and I had seen, as we had suspected, that there was no star.

~

I placed that information in the back of my mind, where it sat, on an open shelf, during the eulogies and the rest of the service and during the gravesite ceremony, as I watched the casket being lowered into the ground, and as I shoveled my spadeful of dirt over it—where the star should be. That absence felt like a final failure of my attention, my vigilance, my intuiting what my father needed or wanted and getting it for him. The absence of the star still sat on that open shelf at the back of my mind, later, at my house, where far fewer people than I'd arranged food for arrived to eat the tea sandwiches and fruit and cheese the caterer I'd hired had set up—mostly my friends, and not those who remained of my father's old friends, further proof of our tangential connection to the community, however kindly it had been. The missing star was still there when everyone left, sooner than expected, and my family and I bagged and froze enough sandwiches to last a month. It was still there when the five of us played Monopoly and Boggle the next day, teasing each other and laughing, as if this were a vacation visit. Then, on Sunday morning, the children were gone, and I became a 63-year-old-Jewish-atheist-only-child orphan, surprising myself by busily brooding about that star.

~

In my mind I revisited the funeral home with my daughter, drove past the statue of Christ as Good Shepherd with His flock on the lawn, took in the "last home" decorousness of polished mahogany furniture, quiet vases with waxy flowers that wouldn't shed pollen on the powder-blue carpet. Holding hands, my daughter and I walked down the hall to the office where the nervous smooth agent awaited us. We chose the casket with the star. Then, holding hands, we went into the "refrigeration room" to see him-not-him, wrapped like a mummy in a tight pale-yellow blanket.

Next, I revisited the following day in my mind. I had gone, by myself, to pay, and to check the details of the little star-adorned booklet, "In Memory," that was to be printed for everyone at the services. I spoke with Mr. K., an agent higher in the hierarchy than Mr. H. Surprising myself, I chose "passed away," rather than the forthright atheist's "died." But I also rejected "gone to his rest," which seemed more euphemistic than "passed away," and, somehow, culturally more Christian (though I found out, after Googling the phrase, that it was also standard in Jewish memorial prayers). Mr. K. told me that he himself was adopted and later learned his birth family was Jewish.

"Has that affected you?" I asked.

"Oh, no, I'm still Catholic," he said, "but it makes me more interested in the Jewish service."

Perhaps more interested than myself, I thought—the unbelonging unbelonger.

On Sunday night I telephoned the funeral home. The nervous smooth agent was, surprisingly, available, and immediately sounded repentant, as if he'd been thinking about that casket all weekend.

"There was some kind of mix-up with regard to that casket, uh—an ordering problem," he mumbled. "Maybe there's something we can do for your family."

"What did you have in mind?" I asked, mentally registering, with a sense of irony, that I probably sounded like a stereotypical version of "my" people.

"Well, it's probably best if you talk to Mr. K. when he comes in tomorrow morning."

Monday morning, I called to speak to Mr. K.

"I don't think there *was* a star present on the exterior of the casket you chose, as pictured in the catalogue. I looked in the catalogue and I did not perceive a star."

"But Mr. K! Mr. H., my daughter, and I took that catalogue to the window and we *all* saw a star."

"I'm going to investigate this. I'll get back to you."

On Tuesday morning, Mr. K. called back.

"The thing is, the problem was refrigeration. A refrigerated casket (that is, when the deceased is not embalmed) could not have had an affixed star because the glue could not withstand the refrigeration."

"That's very odd, Mr. K., because when my mother was at this very mortuary, ten years ago, she was not embalmed, and her casket had a star." I rushed on. "Perhaps it was a metal and not a wood star? Would that have made the difference in the adhesiveness of the glue? It was very clear that my daughter and I had chosen a casket with a star, and it was also very clear that my father was not going to be embalmed. *If* the presence of the star was contingent upon embalming, surely it was contingent upon your agent to inform us of that fact?"

What *did* they think? Was Jew*ish*, unlike Catho*lic*, Protes*tant*, Bap*tist*, Method*ist*, only amateur*ish?* Our symbol negligible, optional?

~

The star had become a cause célèbre in my head, linked to a surprising paranoia about minorities being swept into the majority—those who need no identifying crucifixes on their caskets, because their identity is the null case. Perhaps the *cause* was connected to my need to declare publicly my solidarity with this group I didn't feel so solid with because, in a nation of churchgoers, I was only Jewish*ish*. Perhaps the *cause*—though it could hardly be retroactively dealt with—was motivated by my desire to make up for my own wobbly identity with a gesture immediately to be buried (literally), and to do so in the safe, all-Jewish environment of the temple. Perhaps the star symbolized *something* I thought I could choose and control in this ceremony now so quickly over. Perhaps it was a last debt I still owed my muchloved father that he could now never collect.

"Your agent, incidentally, did ask if there was anything the funeral home could do for my family," I reminded Mr. K., heading precipitately down that "stereotypical" road.

"I'm sorry. Is there anything we can do for you?"

"What did you have in mind?"

"We'll keep you in our prayers."

On Wednesday morning, Mr. K. called again.

"I found out what happened to the star. It was placed on your father's chest."

His shield after all. But what? Like some secret Jew—a Marrano? Watertight alibi. I wasn't going to dig him up.

~

Almost a week later, Mr. K. called again. He had received my grit-teeth letter, written and rewritten over several days, which detailed the *honorable* course of fessing up I thought the funeral home should have taken, and the shock of discovering in the midst of the funeral that the symbol was missing. He "appreciated the letter."

"We made an error," he said. "I am truly sorry."

There was a pause.

"Would you feel better if we made a donation to the temple gift shop in your father's name?" Mr. K. was asking.

I sighed deeply, feeling some understanding had passed between us, feeling both a certain charitableness and a certain dignity. A small window opened up in my understanding of the idea of *compensation*.

"Yes," I said. "I think that would be *most* appropriate."

My claim on the star had been registered. I could let it go.

I heard the silence then, and moved into it: the long silence of my father's death.

Miracles of the Kingdom of Sleep

I.

In a daughter's dream her dead father
lifts a putrid leg (she thinks *I must
take him back to the doctor*) into the pants
of a "restraint suit" she had to buy ($58.95!)
so he would pee into his diaper
(he turns for her, she buttons up
the back) like a good boy, and not unzip
in the middle of the retirement home
dining hall. His flaccid forearms—
islanded with sores—shake
when he punches his own meds
out of bubble packs, with trembling,
fierce fingers. Then he kicks
his wheelchair away like a penitent
at Lourdes. Now he's cruising
the dining hall aisles, glad-handling
the gents, slapping their backs; talking again,
he's soft-talking the ladies
in Alzheimer tongues. He twirls his pearly
handlebar moustache and she is sailing
on the prow of his bike. He soldiers
his shoulders back and she is riding them
into the breakers, her cheek laid
on the ebony waves of his hair,
his arm clasping her legs, the two of them
an ocean-cleaving figurehead. Now
she knows: he has hoisted
the coffin lid and muscled through six feet
of dirt. Her heart swells,
unfurls, and skims.

II.

In a granddaughter's dream, her grandfather
wings down on the day of his funeral
like a Chagall bridegroom, flexes
his feet like a landing crow's,
and screeches to a flailing stop, with a little extra
hop. "Whew!" he winks, so not dead,
and signature squeezes her hands
inside his. They're enclosed
like the innermost Russian doll.
"You baby me too much!" he says,
and commandeers her limo
for a jaunt far, far from school.

At her mother's home, the funeral meats
are growing cold, or warm—
mini-knishes, pickled herring, lox on a dot
of cream cheese on a melba round,
melt-in-your-living-mouth
brie—since

at Temple Beth Zion, the rabbi's prayer books
snooze on the empty coffin, the rabbi,
gritting his teeth, paces
in front of the bimah, slapping a palm
on a thigh, and all the ancient nodders and dodderers,
the limpers and tremorers fidget
in their seats; the cousins
flown in from the East snore—
mouths agape; the great-uncle
who suddenly surfaced twiddles
his wizened thumbs.

How embarrassing!
The dreaming girl
smiles inside the dream,
then laughs out loud.

Half-Deaf, Half-Adjusted

I lost the hearing in my left ear, suddenly, on an agonizingly dizzy morning, November 1, 2000, and it became clear, after ten or so days, that though the dizziness had begun to resolve, my hearing was not coming back. Thus, I didn't have "labyrinthitis," which also can cause a bout of close-to-unbearable dizziness but does not ultimately cause loss of hearing. With all aural information from the left side of my body abruptly blotted out, I went into a period of anger and utter dislocation that I'm sure is involved, initially, in any bodily loss. The anxiety was compounded by uncertainty about the diagnosis. Did I indeed have "sudden hearing loss," a medical term that was woefully indicative of how little doctors knew or could do about this condition, but which was likely to be a single, albeit somewhat rare event, with no statistical implications for the hearing in my other ear? Or might I turn out to be the extremely rare case—the person with "sudden hearing loss" in both ears? (Would I have to learn sign language? Would my family agree to learn it as well? My daughter promised she would.) Or did I possibly have some form of Ménière's disease, another inner ear disorder, which often affected *both* ears, and involved recurrent and unpredictable attacks of dizziness that were accompanied by partial, albeit usually temporary loss of hearing? Ménière's attacks could be mild and infrequent, and even go away on their own, but they could also be so frequent and debilitating as to make it impossible to work, indeed so severe the sufferer would suddenly drop to the floor (as I almost had, on that first day of what turned out to be three days of agonizing vertigo, when the floor of my own bedroom tilted up 45 degrees). The mere threat of having to "adjust" to what can't be adjusted to—the totally random—made my heart race. The doctor, having seen many worse afflictions, shrugged; neither Ménière's nor "sudden hearing loss" was *cancer*. *Be happy.* The audiologist, verifying "profound" loss, explained, when asked, that a conventional hearing aid was out of the picture: "The amplification required would be so great, your head would shake off your neck."

All I could hear out of my left ear, after the doctor's belatedly administered dose of prednisone—which sometimes arrests the inflammation that is perhaps due to a virus, and thus saves all or some hearing—was the highly distorted bass note rumble of the occasional truck, almost worse than the nothing I heard before the prednisone. Nevertheless, I opted for "sudden hearing loss." Yes, that was the one I wanted. The more I read about other possibilities on the all-too-available internet, the more I almost longed for definitive "sudden hearing loss." Ultimately, I would become grateful that it was indeed "sudden hearing loss." But first I had to get used to having it, had to let the body and brain and mind begin their adaptive processes. When the body one takes for granted plays a dirty trick, six weeks—I've come to the conclusion—is the minimal time it takes before one stops feeling totally "abnormal."

For at first, during that rage and dislocation, the altered body feels simply insupportable. It's a little bit like having water in your ear after you've gone swimming, or having a popcorn kernel between your molars when you come home from the movies. You keep on shaking your head, or your tongue keeps trying to extricate that annoying bit of grain. You can't be comfortable until the water or the kernel is gone; you can't be *yourself*. You want it *out*. Making my awareness of abnormality that much more unavoidable was the *tinnitus*—apparently often the result of inner ear disturbances—in the affected ear; I felt as though an enormous noisy conch shell were clamped to my head. The sound invaded silence and would not let me sleep at night. I remember feeling as if I would jump out of my skin; I wanted to shake myself out of myself. I raged against the universe and my husband, because they couldn't *do* anything. I ran out of the house and raced around the block, as if I could run away from my body—barely prevented from screaming by my last remaining shreds of social inhibition.

~

It is a slow process by which the afflicted, estranged body once again becomes one's own. Or, perhaps, the affliction, gradually accepted, becomes part of a reconstituted self. I bought a "white-noise" machine, and was grateful for the mechanically generated sound of waves or rain (mostly I chose rain since waves were too much like what I was trying to blot out) that allowed me to sleep some at night, to escape from the "not me" that pursued me, until, as I finally learned would happen, the brain or mind somehow adjusted to the tinnitus. I no longer hear it, unless something makes me think about it again—as writing about it does now. It's there, but not usually foregrounded in my consciousness.

At first, in spite of the over-the-counter anti-motion sickness drug I was taking on the advice of the doctor, I had to hold on to the walls as I walked in the buildings of my university, forcing myself to make my way to the classrooms in which I taught. The doctor encouraged me to wean myself from the drug, which I soon accomplished; he was right, the brain somehow compensates for the damage to the balancing mechanism the inner ear disorder has caused. But even though my brain's adjustment meant a lessening of my dizziness, it was shocking and distracting to my mind to hear nothing on the far left side of my classroom unless I turned my head, to feel that students speaking from the last rows of a long room were in a silent movie, to pick up no student whispers that allowed me to gauge the reactions in the room, to have to fully look up when students spoke in order to understand them, and thus not be able to glance down at my notes at the same time as I listened to what they said. A constant meta-discourse of split-second decisions played in my head, e.g. *do I ask this mumbling student to repeat his comment for a second time, so I can be sure I got it, or did I get it well enough to move on to the next student's comment which might refer back to his?* My teaching rhythms were discombobulated. If I didn't watch myself, I would become completely and irrationally absorbed by the silence on my left side (as if focusing on it might actually yield faint sounds), or by the chatter inside my own head, and completely miss what my students were saying, or fail to plot my own comments to keep the conversation going. And when a student spoke when my head was down—since I no longer had the aural equivalent of binocular vision—I couldn't locate the source of the sound, and that in itself threw me off track. *Who said that?* Soon it became a joke I had to foster: "If my head flails about trying to locate who said something, please raise your hand!" There *was* something comic about the way I now interpreted sounds I couldn't locate in space; it seemed odd, for example, that my dog was barking *very* rhythmically in some other part of the house as I squeegeed clean my glass shower door after showering—until I stopped squeegeeing and the "barking" also stopped.

But this deep dislocation, the abnormality of my physical self and my sudden mental self-consciousness in an environment to which I had been acclimated for decades, was exhausting. It made me look for refuge to situations that felt as close to the "normal past" as possible. I was happiest, once I began to get over the rage of my initial response, when I was working in my own quiet study, attending to my own thoughts without having to deal with any inputs of sound except for the close clicking of the computer keyboard, the purr of the hard drive, the various beeps and bells. Or when I sat in our small den, watching TV or a movie. When I was in this quiet room, by myself, listening, the volume adjusted to my needs, I could forget that my body had been changed.

Not so outside where beeping horns, rumbling tires, cawing crows refused to locate themselves, or snuck up on me. Especially not so in any remotely social situation. Several times, I was studying the shelves in the supermarket, my cart in the aisle, when someone behind me, irritated that she couldn't get by, jounced the cart or made a pissed-off sound or remark I finally heard; she had been trying to get my attention for half a minute with no success. Not the place to explain one's personal health history, usually. All too easy to feel poutingly sorry for one's self, falsely accused! Since hearing loss is not in any way "visible"— and that's a blessing *and* a liability—even the most well-intentioned people forget that one has it. Just a couple of weeks after that strange morning of sudden loss years ago, when the tinnitus was still an unignorable roar in my ear, I was shopping with a good friend in a department store and we got separated. I could not hear her call me, and I wandered about in an increasingly panicked haze until stumbling into her by accident. "You really *can't* hear, can you," was her comment.

The bigger the group of people, at dinner parties or barbecues, or restaurants, the greater the din of background noise, the more intimidated I felt. Inviting more than a couple of people to dinner at my house, or throwing parties of my own, not to mention going to other peoples', began to feel more like a chore than a pleasure. The only person I could have a real conversation with was the person on my right and I would have to lean in really close, which conveyed a seriousness of focus, a gravity of purpose, that was dull and heavy and not befitting my self-image as a witty conversationalist. And even then, there was bound to be a certain amount of merely social smiling and nodding when I didn't have a clue what the last thing said had been, since breaking into the rhythm of someone's conversational riff to ask for a repeat, is so often like making a completely wacko meta-comment (e.g. "Do you know that the eyeliner on your left eyelid is three times thicker than the eyeliner on your right?"). When I did ask for clarification from some of my dearest friends, it was as if a lightbulb went on in their heads and they began to talk *v-e-r-y* slowly and VERY loudly and both of us were suddenly debilitatingly focused on the medium and not the message.

And ah, eavesdropping—at the student commons or the local grill—that wonderful source of the information we all crave (and writers especially crave) about the mysteries of other lives, was a goner. And it was so clearly no longer possible to listen to two conversations at once, when I could hardly hear all of one. How I missed the social dance of picking up a ribbon of someone's conversation and dancing away with it, then dancing away with a new ribbon and partner. I felt, rather, like I was trying to drop into a conversation by hoisting myself onto one of those thick ropes we had to latch onto for "fire drill" in my college dorm decades ago. By the time I gathered the courage to grab hold, and started my awkward descent, the drill was over.

~

Now, seven years after the onset of my "sudden hearing loss," I am at a dinner after the first day of an academic conference; my husband is a visiting professor at the University of Oslo for a couple of months and I've come to Norway because we have always done things together in our long married life, because I was able to get an unpaid quarter's release from my teaching job, and because a couple of months in a new setting seemed like an ideal time and place to write. A tagalong, I kind of hid out at the conference, sitting at one end of a long table, since the speakers were all connected to the social sciences and I am not. I was careful to insert my "cross" hearing-aid (a device that transmits sound goes into my left, non-hearing ear; a device that picks up the sound goes into my right close-to-normal ear) before starting out for the conference, though I don't wear it very often—partially because I spend a lot of time alone in my study (still more comfortable in silence with my own thoughts than straining for others' words), whether at home in California, or now, in Norway; partially because it doesn't help that much. It amplifies only very slightly on the assumption that the wearer's good ear doesn't require amplification. In a relatively quiet situation, it gives a bit of the illusion that I can hear on my left side, helping me to talk to friends prior to a lecture in an auditorium, for example, when there is only a low buzz of other conversation, and helping me to hear the speaker a bit better once the lecture has begun. Marginal utility. At the conference—which was conducted in English—since the room was quiet, I could hear a fair part of what was being said. But occasionally, a speaker's Norwegian accent was thick enough, or his voice low enough, or he spoke down into his neck, and I was shocked again, as if for the first time, by how quickly the phonemes of English became unrecognizable and failed to combine into words, breaking up, instead, like a pixelating picture, by how easily missing bits of acoustic information turned the flow of words into sludge. There was one conference speaker who used a cane somewhat laboriously to get to his seat and whose voice was especially low and slurred. His arm and hand seemed a bit wobbly, too; perhaps he had suffered a stroke. I could not make out *anything* he said. My husband seemed to have a little bit of difficulty, too, but, clearly, the whole talk was not a wash, for him.

It is this gentleman who sits down next to me, on my left side, at one of the tables, in the too-warm, noisily buzzing dining room, after the conference is over for the day. My husband is on my right, actively engaged in conversation with a man across from him. The man across from me is actively engaged in conversation with the woman on his right directly across from the wobbly gentleman. The voice I hear and comprehend most completely is my husband's, directly on my right, if I attend to it. The acoustics in the room are probably pretty bad for everyone; what I hear is a deafening (ha!) roar that grows worse when I focus on it, and has the emotional effect of approaching rapids towards which my lone canoe is swiftly accelerating. This gentleman on my left introduces himself and offers his hand; I turn completely around to my left to take and shake his hand, and introduce myself. His hand is lax; ah, he *has* probably had that stroke. It is somehow comforting that he offers the affected hand; he is already revealing something about himself, an imperfection—no effort to hide it—and that may make it possible for me to reveal my own imperfection, which is probably going to be something I *have* to do anyway, because eating requires facing the table, but listening to him requires swiveling my head on my neck a full 90 degrees to my left.

It is not socially possible to suggest that we switch seats, which would also require that we switch our already touched food-laden plates, silverware and napkins, even though doing so would ameliorate my difficulties. What an awkward imposition that would be on a complete stranger who is also clearly physically vulnerable (and perhaps the other guests who knew him and his condition would raise their eyebrows). So here I am, turning my head 90 degrees towards a dinner companion, shaking his wobbly hand (later I will find out he has multiple sclerosis, and not stroke-induced weakness), in my hale, mutable, reconstituted, already beginning-to-be-exhausted-from-the-effort state.

~

Looking at him, I understand again, intellectually, and briefly, that returning to "normal" is temporary, that "normal" is a very moveable feast. Our bodies will betray us; we will become grateful for less and less. I tell him, very soon—something in his demeanor besides his disability seeming to make it fairly easy—that I have no hearing at all in the ear closest to him and am wearing a hearing aid that doesn't really help much. He says he has hearing problems too, but refuses an aid, which I take to mean he can hear me a lot better than I him, and maybe that he doesn't fully comprehend the extent of my loss. Clearly it is *way* too late to suggest trading places, were I even able to overcome my inhibitions about such a suggestion. There are swatches of conversation that go by when I nod and smile, quite uncertain what he has said. My neck is becoming sore from my constant turning of it. Yet we do talk, about Norway, about Japan—in which he has a special interest—and about politics in the U.S. I am hungry and would like to take some more bites of my chicken, but am afraid to lose the connection if I look at my plate. Sometimes, as I turn back to him, after daring to take a bite of food, I have to put my left hand on his shoulder to soften the request that he repeat what he has just said, which acknowledges that I haven't really heard a bit of the train of sentences he has just uttered. He asks me what I do, and then what my inspiration is. I tell him about my various chancy, could-turn-out-any-way habits of courting the muse, about how much revision is involved. "Nothing is easy," he says, his hand shaking as he tries to wipe a crumb of bread from his mouth. "It's that way for me, too."

Chronic This and That

Body that drags at me
like an enormous ridiculous
parade balloon that won't
float—goofy-nosed,
wide-eyed, useless—needing
all these handlers
to wrangle it, bouncing
and wobbling, stubbing
its stumpy toes, careening
into barriers, blocking out
huge swaths
of the horizon:

cut your strings,
lighten, rise, so I may
be (oh bodily comfort)
heedless
of body—not a boulder damming
the flowing stream,
a burr catching up
the mind, a seed
in the teeth.

The Two Coasts of the Mind

Another trip to the by now extremely familiar geography of our children's homes and towns outside of D.C. concluded, and I begin to understand what it must be like to live in two (or more) places or landscapes at once—a life I previously associated only with the wealthy who have homes in different time zones and even hemispheres. This time we went in the still temperate fall, blazing with golds that seemed to lighten and ascend, improbable oranges and unlikely rosy reds, and I fell in love again with the grace of trees, their stately promenade down suburban streets, the wispy or blustery rhythms of their falling leaves—always something to feed the eyes, a kinesis in the air giving shape to the wind. So we move, several times a year, from the desert climate of our inland Southern California town, with its unimpeded big sky and often brilliant light, its huge temperature drops from day to night, its crisp or blasting dryness, to the often cloud-locked skies of Maryland, the wan sun of winter, the moister and softer air of spring or fall or the claustrophobically humid air of summer, and to smaller vistas, topped by a hill, descending into a busy road. And, it seems, smaller parking lots that take considerable maneuvering, smaller—or cozier?—stores that are crowded more hours of the day.

The rhythm of living—if for very unequal periods of time—in two places, living, as opposed to being a tourist, i.e. going to the grocery store, washing clothes, taking out the trash, is relatively new to me. Our children have only been settled in the D.C. area—because of their jobs—for a few years. Many of the prior landscapes of my life were ones I more permanently left behind, closed books. My anthropologist husband and I lived in Ghana for fifteen months, decades ago, when he was doing his fieldwork for the PhD; we've never returned. After that we lived in a suburb of Oxford, England, for about nine months, when I researched my own PhD dissertation at the Bodleian Library; we've passed through Oxford since, but never *lived* there again— dangerously using a space heater to take the chill off the bathroom in our uninsulated and unheated apartment when we bathed, typing notes with gloves on, keeping one package of Birds Eye frozen peas in the minuscule freezer of the minuscule fridge, buying Cornish pasties at the bakery for weekend lunches.

Going back and forth several times a year, from the landscape of our lives in Southern California to another familiar but different landscape feels a bit like moving between places in the mind or heart. Although I grew up farther North in an apartment building in densely populated New York City rather than in a house in a pleasant suburb like the ones my children live in, the Eastern look of houses, vegetation, skies, the Eastern weather, make me feel that I am revisiting the scene of my childhood which has gradually slipped South. And going back at the peak of the turning leaves, rather than, say, at the height of summer, when to breathe is to swallow tiny gnats that swarm in the air, or wipe them from one's nose, permits the indulgence of that feeling. How familiar, how *natural* it feels to be cold in the Eastern cold (and it is different, isn't it, from the Southern California cold to which we have just returned, though the temperature might be almost the same), to be "bundled up," as we said in my childhood, to be too hot indoors, at the Starbucks, behind steamed windows, in our winter coats and scarves. How resonant the sound of the scrape of rakes (but wait, the leaves from the few trees on my Bronx street just blew away, or were they dealt with by the building superintendent, or the street cleaners?), the dry fingers of the leaves skipping down the sidewalk, the rustle and creak of branches outside my window (but wait, there are trees on my street in my inland Southern California town, in front yards, if not on the street's verge—olives, pines, silk floss, cedar), how deeply rooted in the chest the sadness of that pale, pale sun obscured by thick cloud batting ...

When we return to LAX, the streets seem so unprotected, so bare and there, so unmellowed by trees, not the way they looked when we left. And, then, the next morning, I walk out onto my deck at home: how fragrant and balmy the air is, how light I am in my tee shirt, jeans and flip-flops, how freeing is the sun.

Minding Desert Places – Winter, 4 P.M.

Shadows lay themselves down
on the bare hills, darkly
soft, breast to breast.

Every tree and bush
in the wash—mesquite,
creosote, tamarisk—
is articulate
in its loneliness.

Cholla blink here,
there, guttering out.

Light slides from the warm
rock's upturned face.

You still see nothing
that is not there,
but now you sense everything
that is.

Blue Bowl of Sky

How we feel about where we are, what our mental image is of the weather and landscape of our days, depends on where we were before, and how we arrived.

I first saw the West of small towns and desert spaces when, very young, and only a few months married, my husband and I drove from the East Coast to start graduate school in Northern California which we approached circuitously, via the Southwest, where he had already been, and where there were Native American ruins he wanted me to see and friends he wanted me to meet. New York City, the densest, most highly urban landscape in the U.S., had been the seemingly infinite center of my childhood and young adult world; when we drove west, I left behind my entire family—parents, aunts, uncles and cousins—in the Bronx, Queens, Manhattan and "the Island." Though the generation above me were almost all immigrants from Europe, only one of them or their children had been as far as Michigan; most hadn't been west of Pennsylvania.

My husband and I were in that stage of life when buying Melmac plates in beige and aqua at a drugstore—our first dinner service!—was exciting. An only child, marrying and venturing to the edge of the continent, I was shaking off the yoke and protection of my loving but intensely close parents (which I had begun to loosen when I chose to go to college in Massachusetts, though my mother had preferred that I stay in "the city.") All that first year of graduate school—in those pre-email, pre-cell phone days, when long- distance calls (considered too expensive for everyday talk) meant someone had died—my dad sent tapes for me to play on a cheap tape recorder, lugubrious tapes about how much he and mom missed me, his voice thick with incipient tears.

On that first trip to the far West, it was both strange and exhilarating to see towns whose beginnings and endings were visible—compared to the seeming endlessness of building-crowded New York avenues—towns whose dusty streets dropped off into the desert, vulnerable, unprotected, yet brave towns, rubbing up on vast silences. I first saw forests with solitary, articulate pines in receding rows, no fuzzy, obscuring understory—only pine needles—on the ground between them; I liked that independence and clarity. And most of all in that September, once we'd crossed the Rockies, I saw an unobscured horizon; even the suburban and rural parts of the Northeast were so much less panoramic than Western vistas; I saw sky. This was a sky no longer white, close, and hovering; it was as if a great gauze bandage had been lifted from my sight. This sky was an enormous bowl of blue turned over, drenching us in light, dropping out a bit of horizontal detritus: a town, a gas station on an empty road, a collection of rocks.

Of course, there had been days in New York when the ocean breezes cleansed the air and it was brisk and crystalline. And, of course, every kind of New York weather was the weather of my childhood and therefore, in my childhood, weather as weather should be. But the horizon in Manhattan (where I went to high school) is devoured by and textured with buildings; the eye is drawn to detail opening onto more detail: walls of glass reflecting sky and cloud, windows capturing and throwing the discus sun. Even outside Manhattan, in the provincial Bronx where I was raised, apartment houses crowd the sky; the eye alights on their crenellated tops, on the aerials stuck like haphazard pins in the pincushions of their tarry roofs. The buildings hold one in like the walls of slot canyons; vistas plunge down them. The sky may be infinitely melancholy at dusk, but it seems to be made that way by the lights coming on in innumerable apartment windows. It is juxtaposed, always, for me, to the mass and might of human architecture, to the vast collection of human souls buzzing tightly in one place. My young husband and I had driven out under a sky that was boss or god, under an enormous blue bowl where the wind blows without restriction. And after that first trip across the United States, I lived in a new mental space, a new psychological weather, even though the Northern California town near our university, where we rented an apartment during our first year, looked surprisingly seedy for blue and golden California. That unconfined wind seemed to sweep even the slightly cloying familiarity of my natal family from me. I was new when I stepped off the plane on the next summer visit East, into the white haze of air, air palpable on my shoulders as my mother's hand—which I would now tolerate—brushing some lint from my jacket that I hadn't asked to be brushed.

I lived in that space, even if—when my husband got a job in inland Southern California—I was shocked by the aridity and heat of September, the sky and mountain obscuring smog, especially because he had given me an idyllic verbal scratch and sniff with greenery and orange blossoms after his visit the previous May. And I continued to live in that psychological weather system, a blue-gold near desert sparkle, during all the years I drove weekly on the 215 between Iowa Avenue and Mill Street to do my shopping at Fedco—that nude expanse of dusty freeway blowing with trash, unsoftened by trees or grassy median, and, like many Southern California freeways, much uglier than many Eastern highways.

Now I have lived here for decades; my parents have grown old and died; my children have grown up and flown. And even now, when there are more and wider freeways—certainly no prettier—there are days of sky, perhaps especially in the early spring when it is not yet too hot and orange blossom is in the air (at least on the university campus), when my mental weather, that Platonic ideal, is realized in the actual, sublunary world. I feel exalted, unleashed, grateful, lost in that cloudless blue that makes me crane my head back to take it in, as if I could never get tired of it, never want argosies of cumulus, or sky-texturing cirrus. It has depth and no depth at the same time. It is a blue so profound it seems to burn, so pure it seems the archetype of the celestial. My head so far back I am dizzy, I look at and into the sky, feeling unadulterated joy, however briefly feeling free.

Ex-New Yorker Remembers Her Natural Landscape

Fortress city—
houses cresting ridges
like battalions of horses,
battlements of near tenements—
flaming suns leaping
from window to window ...

Tree house city—how shocking my first sight
of western towns, like knots in the ribbon
of the road, sediment in the cup
of sky

Infinite city—shocking their visible limits
crumbling into desert,
compared to your manifold crannies,
unvisited planets,
your range after dimly inhabited
range fuzzing into blue like mountains,
and beyond those your faint white
blur like cloudy space dense
with stars

Intimate city—greasy as dirt
under my nails, close as soot
on my eyelashes, as the secret odors
of plebeian and patrician thickening
in public washrooms, as their voices twanging
down my spine, spilling
entire histories, descents into hell,
recoveries

Vertiginous city—from your highest towers
other buildings lose
their moorings; thousands
of lanterns on swaying
ropes rock out of a fog

and far below, five o'clock tides
of dusky forests surge forward,
each tree moated by its inner
silence

and night falls fast,
so fast, piling up in steep
soft drifts, canceling
cornice, column, piling up
in streets of ash and embers

Oh, my city of sorrows

From Bagels, via George Herbert's *Temple*, to OMG! the Temple

Snapshot, 1956: I am 12 or 13, sitting by my bedroom window on the fifth floor of our Bronx apartment building, which overlooks the roof of an Orthodox synagogue. It is a Saturday morning, and the low buzz and occasional soaring wail of the men davening next door fill the air, so familiar as almost not to be noticed. I am reading Homer Smith's *Man and His Gods*, in part a diatribe against the suffering caused by and violence committed in the name of religion throughout history, a book lent to me by my then very liberal favorite uncle, a sort of Christopher Hitchens, avant la lettre. My mother has gone with her shopping cart over the cracked sidewalks to the bakery a few blocks away on 161st Street, where the customers are probably four-deep in rows behind the counter. Maybe she will buy some rugelach, or poppyseed strudel, or some mandelbrot, or a chocolate marble babka, along with the bagels and bialys and the salt sticks for Sunday morning breakfast. The very air is thickly immigrant Jewish on 161st Street, redolent with cadence and accent. It is absorbed through the pores, whether you know anything about Judaism as a religion or not.

~

Snapshot, 1959: I have "cut" the obligatory Friday night services at a religious summer camp in Northern New York State and am hanging out, chatting about my anti-religious feelings with the equally inclined camp doctor, who is 24, and, outrageously, smoking—in both the literal and slang senses. I have, by then, overheard too many conversations about whether you can or cannot pick up a pen, say, from a chair, on the Sabbath, if you want to sit down on said chair. In my sixteenth summer, my mother has inflicted this observant Jewish camp on me because her revered and conservative elder brother chose it for my suburban cousin. My mother often compares her favorably to me; my aspiring-to-beatnik self of course finds her too bourgeois. My immigrant mother's Judaism is domestic and social or political. She maintains a kosher home and creates High Holiday and Passover meals with the full panoply of restrictions. She is a fierce advocate of Israel. She is sure she can separate the Jews from the goyim we meet on the street by looks alone. She worries about "what is good for the Jews"; apparently black-suited Hasidim are not. But, as far as I can remember, she has not set foot in a synagogue, except for her good friend's son's bar mitzvah, when we went as a family. Whether that is because she and my more skeptical and less chauvinist, but equally hardworking father don't have the inclination or the leisure, or don't have the money for dues, I don't know. Way back, in the early grades, I was sent to Sunday school in another synagogue around the corner, but I didn't like it, and, indulgently, my mother and father did not force their only child to stay.

~

Snapshot, 1963: It is the era of intense study of texts, the New Criticism is in full glory, and I am intently studying John Donne's Holy Sonnets, every fricative and sibilant, in an English class on the seventeenth-century metaphysical poets at Smith. What am I feeling when I read, in the sestet of "If poysonous mineralls, and if that tree": "Oh! of thine onely worthy blood," and I hear that repeated wailing long "o" and the soul-wringing strain in "ONely WORthy"?[12] What am I feeling when I read George Herbert's urgent paradoxes of rebellion, love and utter abjection in *The Temple*?

> Well, I will change the service, and go seek
> > Some other Master out.
> Ah my deare God! Though I am clean forgot,
> Let me not love thee, if I love thee not.
> > "Affliction (I)"[13]

Whatever it is, it has something to do with my monastic devotion to poetry, and the kind of hushed concentration involved in saying and hearing every syllable. It has something to do with willed and deep involvement in the emotional trajectories of these Christian poems in which I've been asked—as part of my *literary training*, which is, in turn, a sort of unacknowledged passport to a wider, and more socially elite world—to immerse myself. Later, I will write an award-winning honors thesis on another priest-poet of whom I become enamored, the Jesuit Gerard Manly Hopkins. To study literature is to study Christianity, although this is never overtly said. And, truth be told, it is not especially foregrounded in my mind, either. Nor does anyone ever remotely broach the question of the emotions involved, especially for those who are not Christian. Even this, my compartmentalizing, conscious mind seems, at least momentarily, to ignore. Almost five decades later, I will publish a poem about my youthful "experiencing" of even anti-Jewish Christian poetry in accordance with the reigning critical approach:

The Heresy of Paraphrase

> *A true poem is ... an experience rather than any mere statement about experience.*
>
> —Cleanth Brooks, *The Well-Wrought Urn*

Spit on my face you Jewes, and pierce my side,
I intone, an acolyte in the garden
of study—Jewish girl from the Bronx
on scholarship at an Ivy college—
kneeling before the vaunted poem.
I am imagining John Donne
imagining the crucifixion, meditating

in my carrel-retreat above
the snow-hushed dorms—as Louis Martz said
Donne meditated with the help
of the *Spiritual Exercises of Saint
Ignatius Loyola* in *The Poetry of Meditation*
(Yale U.P., 1954). Toes freezing
in my boots, I give myself
to the text, artifact holy
as a reliquary, *autotelic*—
that word chanted in reverent tones
by Professor R. who's in love with the swirl
of the Baroque, and swirls with it,
his own turns and bows as beautiful,
he knows, as what he bows to.
I am experiencing every phoneme
like blessed wounds; as Donne
becomes Christ—for *sinnes,*
which passe the Jewes impiety—
I become him, my voice lowering
to his plangent prayer in the sestet—
Oh let mee then … admire—
and not once do I think *Jewes,*
Jews[14]

~

Wedding snapshot: June, 1964. I marry a Southern man I met
at a Hillel college mixer. Bourgeois rented-tails-and-top-hat
two-family brilliance at the Grand Concourse Plaza Hotel,
complete with chazan and ketubah—signed by my father, the
giver, and my husband, the recipient—and finally smashed flash-
bulb, which at first squirts away and has to be chased by the
groom.

~

Snapshot: 1983, skipping along now, time running faster. Brief and rather quickly overcome distress, partially parent-inculcated, over whether our firstborn, our son, almost thirteen—who has never taken Hebrew lessons—should have a bar mitzvah. My mother, now living in a "trial" apartment in our town with my dad, to see if she and he can actually make the cultural leap from New Rochelle to inland Southern California, seems to have a New York model in her head of the "quickie" Bar Mitzvah. But no such opportunities are readily available, though our son, for a nanosecond, considers the benefits of glory and presents. And we really already made that decision ages ago when we didn't enroll him in Hebrew school. His father, although a bar mitzvah himself, was unable to justify the time in a busy kid's life—what with soccer and the elementary school musical in which the kid sang the lead—when he himself couldn't convince himself of "belief." When our daughter approaches thirteen, the question of a bas mitzvah doesn't even come up, though by that time my parents have moved to our town and, for the first time in their adult lives, actually at my suggestion ("you'll meet people, you'll have fun"), have joined the only nearby Jewish place of worship, a Reform Temple to which they occasionally bring their granddaughter, and, very, very rarely, all of us.

~

Snapshots: In the 80s, 90s or 2000s at dinners with friends—almost all happily apostate Protestants or Catholics—connected to the university where we both teach, dinners liberally lubricated with wine. R., talking about her father's strict commitment to an evangelical church she had to attend, cracks us up by calling Jesus, Cheeze-us, making me go hunt up a Lorrie Moore story, "Terrific Mother." The heroine, suffering horrific guilt (because of a freak accident that caused her friend's baby's death) goes for a massage:

Speakers were built into the bottom of the table, and out of them came the sound of eerie choral music, wordless oohs and aahs in minor tones, with a percussive sibilant chant beneath it that sounded to Adrienne like Jesus is best, Jesus is best," though perhaps it was "Cheese, I suspect."[15]

In response to my anthropologist husband's "If I had to choose, I would call myself an agnostic," my novelist friend and I, both dyed-in-the wool atheists, each taking another sip of merlot, say "Oh, no, we *know*." No one has anything at all positive to say about any aspect of religion except another anthropologist who considers himself a believer in all religions and sometimes attends an Episcopal Church, and a woman who recently joined Wicca. A former student is actually distressed: in the process of trying to extricate herself from an abusive relationship, and in the hope of comfort and support, she joined a friend's Baptist church, but, she says, "they get inside your head and set up house." One professor from a Jewish family refuses any connection whatsoever; he thinks of all practicing Jews as being in the Dark Ages. It is only very, very recently that I begin to think: hmm, most of these people are extremely subtle in the distinctions they make in their *academic* work, but they sure can generalize pretty wildly about religion in their private lives.

~

Wedding snapshot: 2003. Our non-practicing Jewish son marries a non-practicing Protestant woman. Our closest totally apostate Protestant friend obtains convenient ordination online through the Universal Life Church and officiates. Émile Durkheim—a father of sociology and anthropology and a proponent of the social origin and function of religion—is invoked, rather than God, during the moving ceremony, written by the major participants.

~

Wedding snapshot: 2008. Our non-practicing Jewish daughter marries a non-practicing Muslim man. A woman Episcopal priest presides—a rabbi or an imam, even if one or the other agreed to officiate, would be problematical—but though the priest speaks of marriage in a way that strongly reminds me of the Anglican *Book of Common Prayer*, she follows the wishes of the bride and groom and does not explicitly invoke God. As in our son's wedding, there is something moving and inspiring about differences bridged by love. Or maybe, in the absence of practice, there are few such differences.

~

Snapshot: Spring 2010. The cathedral in its spacious square, right across from our hotel in Strasbourg, France, where, already retired, we are vacationing for a few days, after a conference my husband attended in nearby Landau, Germany. I think I can imagine something of the embrace of the medieval church, when wattle and daub houses huddled up all around it. The bells ring all day and all night, drawing the town in around the square, shepherding me somewhere in my sleep.

~

Snapshot: Spring 2012. Our daughter, her husband, and his parents, holding our twin grandchildren. Our daughter and son-in-law have gone abroad to visit her husband's parents, who are practicing Muslims. There is, apparently, some sort of naming ceremony for the children involving the slaughtering of a sheep, but we are told it is not a religious ceremony. When we hear this, my husband and I joke that we should slaughter our own sheep, and join the local temple, so we can take the kids to services—to balance their exposure—when they visit with their folks.

~

APARTNESS

Brief video: a Friday evening, August, 2013. My husband and I, newly joined members of our local Reform Temple, are at our first Sabbath services together, and I am very much aware that I have finally come to the place where I sent my long-dead parents all those years ago ("You'll make friends! You'll have fun!"). Whereas my husband's childhood included synagogue services with some regularity, it is probably only the sixth or seventh time in my long life that I have been to Jewish services, and at least two of those times were with my parents, after they joined our local temple, and two at my parents' funerals. My father went along, not without some apparent pleasure, with this revival of religious services in his life (familiar enough from his Orthodox childhood), and participated fully in temple business after they joined, but made clear to me that he was still no believer. My mother enjoyed a few culturally familiar people and the outings the temple sponsored, and rather mysteriously started talking about "belief" in a vaguely fundamentalist way, perhaps because she was beginning to experience the frailties of old age. In their late-blooming temple membership, it was as if my parents took on Judaism so that I didn't quite have to. Whatever attraction I had for the religion was really an extension of my love for them.

Now I am feeling a little like a convert. The bits of awesomeness—the majestic doors of the Ark, the opening and closing of them in the rituals of the service, the Torah scrolls within dressed in their dark blue velvet mantles, adorned with silver crowns, finials and shields, the rhythms of the congregation rising, and sometimes bowing, and reseating itself, the profound soar of the cantor's voice, the sheer Durkheimian act of participating in communal movement, communal lifting of the voice— all this is a little strange and exciting to me. A part of me wonders how soon the newness will wear off and these things become boringly familiar, as I wondered, on those extremely rare times when my husband and I did attend previously—and I had one arm around my mom and one around my dad, all of us swaying—whether my emotions would survive a steady diet of attendance.

~

Stop the camera! How did I come to be the person sitting in this sanctuary; how does this person relate to the person who scorned even agnosticism, saying, "oh, no, I *know*"? I am still an atheist. I definitely do not and cannot believe in a personal, providential God who has created us in his image, who, as the prayer books have it, orders and controls the universe, who makes the seasons alternate, and controls the stars as they travel through the skies, who rolls light away from darkness and darkness from light. I do not believe in a divine power that blesses good and punishes evil. While the universe clearly contains profound mysteries beyond my ken, I cannot believe in some "intelligent design" at work on the whole. And yet I am sitting here, though wondering intermittently whether that makes me a hypocrite, as my husband wondered about the integrity of sending our son to Hebrew school all those years ago. Perhaps those of us not "born into" a religious practice, who don't belong as a matter of course, especially feel a need to "explain," not least, to themselves. When I think about the reasons I am here, I start accumulating the contingent, the mundane, perhaps just some whispers of those inching toward the weightier.

I have been intellectually interested in religion for a long time. My scholarly research, particularly for the book I wrote focused on *King Lear*, took me deeply into the relation of Shakespeare's work to early modern Christian religious controversy. My intellectual interest is undoubtedly in part motivated by my being an outsider with regard to America's dominant Protestant Christianity, as well as an atheist who wonders "How can 'they' 'believe' in such stuff?" and "What does 'belief' mean?" I had briefly met the rabbi of our local Reform Temple when I was invited to give a poetry reading there, and at demonstrations against a Nazi organization that goose-stepped through a section of our town. Our town grapevine buzzed with glowing descriptions of her. My husband and I, having the freedom and time that retirement entails, decided to invite her to discuss with us the shape of a modern religion, particularly Judaism, that would allow, or indeed attract people like ourselves. Perhaps, way behind this overt project, was some half-conscious desire to reevaluate our own relation to Jewish religious practice, but it was not uppermost. We were thinking we might write a book.

Initial contingency. This woman was in another league from the former rabbis I had either encountered briefly or heard of at our local temple. The prior rabbis had apparently been, respectively: interested in social action, but tediously boring; insouciant about their responsibilities, or in fact, immoral—one married rabbi had an affair with a congregant. We met Rabbi V. several times at our house and discussed our anxieties about "organized religion," or, more honestly, mainly mine, since I am the stranger in a strange land, whereas my husband's family went to synagogue frequently enough when he was young to make it something other than a novel experience. We didn't start a book. We kind of fell in love with the rabbi's warmth, openness, and intelligence, her inclusive understanding, and her seriousness. Had she been more like any of the previous rabbis, clearly lesser *people*, we might have immediately thought "uh-oh, no way!"

It was reassuring to hear that many in Rabbi V.'s congregation, and she herself, did not, after all, believe in that anthropomorphic personal God who "rolls light away from darkness and darkness from light." Sometimes "the good" or the possibility of good in the universe was mentioned as a substitute for that personal Deity. I remained nervous: "the good" does not demand worship, but the God of the Old Testament does; how does one *worship* good, or the possibility of good?

I have always felt ethnically or culturally Jewish, though the role of that Jewishness has obviously very much attenuated in my life; I am an intense, excitable, sometimes totally uncool New York Jew, by birthright. I have come to treasure my belonging to a minority, not least because I appreciate the occasional jaundiced eye that minorities may cast on the pieties of the dominant American culture and religion, on the way in which "God" and politics are frequently tied, in spite of the constitution's separation of church and state and of religious persuasion and political office, and I treasure that membership, even if—or especially because—my minority is often cultural, and not religious. But wasn't it true, when one is living in a largely non-Jewish environment, that such a sense of cultural identity—tied only to the recordings my husband and I own of cantorial performances which move me deeply (perhaps that much more *because* of my living outside the culture), or to the occasional Yiddish word that pops, with all its redolence, into a conversation with the rare Jewish friend—can easily crumble, fade, or dissolve into the mainstream—in the absence of practice or study? And my parents were gone; I could no longer piggyback on their almost iconic immigrant Jewishness, or share in their temple membership by proxy, or enjoy a cultural Jewishness that was an offshoot of their lives. What if, in the absence of religious practice, cultural Jewishness becomes so diluted as to, ultimately, disappear? Thus, though I may have suppressed the thought for some time, in response to the rabbi's question, asked without coercion: *Do you care if Judaism completely disappears?* I surprise myself by answering, *Yes, I think I do.*

Nevertheless, my story is hardly a "conversion story," even if I do feel like what I imagine converts feel like at services, at least right now. We do not decide, after our sessions talking with lovely Rabbi V., after becoming friends with her and her husband, after being invited to her house for dinner, and inviting her to ours, that we will join right away. Once the possibility of joining has been planted in our minds, however, and has no obvious immediate impediments such as the somewhat obnoxious rabbis of time past, mulling it around gradually reveals some advantages we hadn't previously focused on.

It's no accident that the population of religions organizations is often slanted towards the long in the tooth. Our official working lives over, we are somewhat isolated. In our case, many of our university friends are retired as well, and so free to travel or visit their far-flung kids, as we do, and are therefore less often around to share a social life with us. Our last frontier lies ahead of us—my husband, in mundane pragmatic mode, points out that we need someplace to have our funerals!—much more obviously ahead of us than when we were working. There is a faint but real comfort, if not exactly a belief in the eternity of spirit, or anything like that, in approaching that frontier in the company of others, on the same train. The doors open, and, as before, some new people board, and some older people step off. The train has traveled this route thousands and thousands of times before and it will again. I imagine that one feels both very small, and, at the same time, accounted for.

Final contingency. My husband has been somewhat phlegmatic all along, or perhaps has been waiting for the impetus from the stickler, his wife. But the tipping point for our decision is what I blush about—the final little psychological push. My brother-in-law, with whom I shared my story, called it "holy bribery." Though I know Rabbi V. was doing nothing like this, I started worrying—and needing a cold wet wash cloth, as my cheeks got hot—that though we've so much enjoyed seeing her and her husband for dinners at her house and at ours, she would be too busy to keep us on her list, if we didn't join her congregation.

So, here I am, on a Friday night in August, my prayer book open, for the moment almost shocked at the God in it, who seems like the Ineffable, the Abstract, the Unknown, and almost shocked at the elegance and simplicity of the language, its failure to offend me. Maybe it is language itself that I am worshipping.

> May the Maker of peace in the high places make peace descend upon us and upon all Israel, and let us say: Amen.
> May the Source of strength, who blessed the ones before us, Help us find the courage to make our lives a blessing, and let us say: Amen.
>
> May the Source of peace send peace to all who mourn and comfort to all who are bereaved. Amen.[16]

My eyes briefly moisten, as they did when I was at services with my parents, because of the attention paid by the language in this place, to what is barely acknowledged in my secular life, but surrounds it. And, literary student that I am, I find myself thinking of the British poet Philip Larkin's 1955 poem, "Church Going," which begins with his persona wandering casually into a church, but only "once [he is] sure there's nothing going on." Although the poem is written squarely from the perspective that churches are defunct, superannuated, it ends with a certain respect for them, as places which once

> held unspilt
> So long and equably what since is found
> Only in separation—marriage, and birth,
> And death, and thoughts of these— ... .

The respect, however qualified, is for the way churches housed the weighty questions of our lives. The poem concludes:

A serious house on serious earth it is,
In whose blent air all our compulsions meet,
Are recognized, and robed as destinies.
And that much never can be obsolete,
Since someone will forever be surprising
A hunger in himself to be more serious,
And gravitating with it to this ground,
Which, he once heard, was proper to grow wise in,
If only that so many dead lie round.[17]

In the temple tonight I am reminded, and it seems the people with me are taking time out from the busyness of their lives to remind themselves, as great literature reminds me, that we live *sub specie aeternitatis*, that life, like the flight of Bede's sparrow through the mead hall, is a passage from darkness to the darkness of which we know nothing, with only a brief interlude of warmth and cheer in-between.

The numerous Protestant tracts and polemics that I read when I was doing literary research (and my small experience of Orthodox Judaism), as well as powerful fiction and memoir, warned me off of religion, but, in a paradoxical way, my long immersion in early modern religious poetry emotionally prepared me for its possibility, laid the groundwork for it.

On the one hand, I think my prior subliminal idea of religion involved something like a constant uneasy test of faith, or of a credo. I thought of those Reformation Calvinist believers in predestination who were constantly on guard, looking for "signs" that they were saved, though I knew that others, convinced of their election, may have been filled with joy, and may have lived in a way that served to prove their blessedness. I thought of the frightening power of the elders in congregations, such as the Massachusetts Bay Colony, to be a scourge on the consciences of those they thought sinners, and of my university friend who experienced something like this firsthand in the present day. I thought of the social pressures brought to bear on the young who were "supposed" to be experiencing their personal call by Christ by a certain age, that I had read about in fiction such as James Baldwin's *Go Tell It on the Mountain* and memoir such as Kim Barnes' *In the Wilderness*. In my "own" religion, insofar as it had a lot of "rules" about the practices of daily life and of worship, like the Orthodox Judaism I was thinly acquainted with, I was afraid of my ignorance, of standing out like a greenhorn.

Yet, on the other hand, my reading of the great poetry of Anglicans like Donne and Herbert, of Catholics like Hopkins, laid down some emotional substructures, almost trained me in feeling gratitude, reverence for life and the world, and joy, though, in the last analysis, I could not completely intellectually ignore the connection of these emotions, in context, to Christian belief and doctrine, which may have ultimately walled them off. Yet I wonder, can these emotions transcend a particular theology? As an undergraduate, was I merely imagining, under the guise of New Critical appreciation of these Christian works as "an experience rather than any mere statement about experience," only Christian struggles of faith, Christian reverence, Christian consolation? I encountered gratitude, reverence, and joy, in poems embedded in a theology descended from, yet different from Judaism's, a theology in which these emotions are so often responses to the Incarnation and to the sacrifice of Christ that makes salvation and eternal life possible. Yet I am not willing to say these poets cannot be read and enjoyed by non-Christians, or that all, or even most of the emotions in their poems are exclusive to Christianity. Perhaps my mind might rationally resist the underlying theology of a poem like Herbert's "The Flower," if I bring it to the fore, but my heart cannot help respond to the joy there in the use of one's gifts, and in recovery from affliction:

And now in age I bud again,
After so many deaths I live and write;
I once more smell the dew and rain,
And relish versing: O my onely light,
It cannot be
That I am he
On whom thy tempests fell all night.[18]

Such poems truly got to me in spite of the barriers surrounding them; I felt them. In some measure, I needed those emotions of joy, reverence, and gratitude; I still need them. These are good emotions; when I experience them in the temple, however fleetingly, I feel cleansed, calm, at peace.

Yet my ardent questions still remain: how can I experience joy in the plenitude of the world, revere its splendors and intricacies and interconnectedness, be grateful for being alive in this moment in time, and for the people in my life, without belief or faith in a Creator, a personal beneficent Giver, an Object of gratitude? Religions are constantly renegotiating their central texts; in many cases what was once understood literally comes to be understood as metaphor. But at some point doesn't the metaphorization need to stop? What is God a metaphor for? How can one worship the tenor of a mere metaphor? Is the comfort I feel at times in the sanctuary, with the congregation, with the words I say and hear thus in any sense specious? Am I involved in New Age "religion lite"?

Or is my asking that question merely a function of my nose-to-the grindstone first-generation American-Jewish personality that believes everything good should require really hard work, abetted by that Protestant model I absorbed—in the absence of real knowledge about Judaism—of the constant, arduous test of faith?

We are all rising now, to go into the social hall for the Oneg. For the moment, I am living in and with the questions.

A Familiar Train of Religious Observances

My grandfathers and grandmothers board
in separate cars. The men hold on
to the leather straps, swaying and mumbling,
heads slightly bowed. The women
swim the air three times with their bent arms,
gathering it toward themselves, then cover their
closed eyes with their palms. Eventually, they get off,
one by one, and disappear into the ether.

My parents, in retirement leisure, board
together. My father plays the sad clown
for the only little kids around, and both run
into his open arms. My mother offers her pruned
parchment cheek to an excessively dressed
and perfumed woman, then kisses her
in return—as if swallowing a stone.
Then everyone sits down.

In the reverie of motion, my father murmurs
syllables he learned by rote as a child,
as did his father; my mother, not wanting
to be left out, moves her lips.
When it's almost time
to disembark, they stand up, arms
around each other—as never at home—
and around the strangers on each side,
swaying. Eventually, they disengage
and step off, one by one, disappearing
into the ether.

You and I, so busy Elsewhere, leap on
just as the doors are closing. We fumble
with the unfamiliar books. The train rocks,
and we lose our places. We rumble into stations
memorializing the names of our grandparents
and parents. It's as if our children
never were.

You bring along your father's
prayer shawl in its sueded bag,
and I, my father's, in its velvet pouch—
as though, if you hood yourself
in that cream and blue, if I cloak myself
in that white and gold, we will each
be recognized, and find arms
to run into, when, at separate times,
lonely, we disembark.

Operating in French

My hunger increased by visions of pain au chocolat and pain aux raisins, I hurried down the staircase of our modest hotel, my Frenchless husband, who had no intention of contributing to the order, some paces behind. We'd awakened quite hungry on this fourth and last morning in Brittany, but had packed our suitcases before considering food. I'd suggested we buy some pastries at the boulangerie just across the street, and enjoy them on our little balcony overlooking the pleasantly scruffy garden, making do with the tea and coffee packets and the small electric teapot in our room. We were leaving as soon as possible for Normandy, where we would join our Foreign Service son and his family for a precious few days—the raison d'être of our relatively short and somewhat last minute trip to France, our most beloved European destination. They had been on their own vacation in Europe, and were making their final stop at a French gîte, a rural vacation home, before returning to his post in Phnom Penh.

No traffic on the little street I began to cross, almost running, eyes to my left on the goal—though, at well over 70, with arthritis in one knee, and a knee replacement in the other, as well as osteoporosis and a history of fractures—followed by long-worn casts—in my last decade and a half, I don't ever *really* run. There was a bay on my left on the far side of the street where shoppers parked their cars, sometimes leaving them with motors on, while they leapt into the boulangerie and out again with their baguettes. Perhaps for that reason I didn't expect the sidewalk to jut out into the street in front of me and to my right; I tripped over the curb, was bowled over by gravity's nonnegotiable shove—the elapsing second long enough for me to think *I can pull myself upright oh no not again*—and my right hand twisted palm skyward, and smashed into the concrete when my body fell on top of it. *Again.* Using my left hand and arm, I somehow got my lower body into a sitting position on the sidewalk; my right hand dripped off its arm like a steak held up by a butcher. The skin was peeled off and pebbles and grit clustered in the bloody open gash. My instincts told me the wrist (at least) was fractured, yet I hoped against hope for a mere deep wound. I held my right arm with my left, and rocked with pain, tears sprouting from my eyes, my husband, now in front of me, shouting "What happened? What happened?" and I felt pitifully embarrassed and chagrined, to have turned, in an instant, from a passably adroit traveler into a doddery American tourist who had plopped into people's lives on this mild French morning on so quiet a French street.

As if summoned directly by my pain and fear, people appeared around us, in action. One man was on his cell making a call, presumably for help. Another, clearly versed in treatment for shock, offered what looked like an old blanket. Our hotel host (summoned by unseen social networks?) quickly strode across the street, and squatting by my side, asked if I wanted an orange juice. I fended off the blanket, approved the juice to come, agreed mentally, without talking to the man on the phone, that whoever he was calling needed to arrive. Catapulted out of our balmy European escape, I was in it now—the emergency, the awkward, annoying, faintly ridiculous situation. Our ample and leisurely dinner the night before at our hotel's restaurant "gastronomique"—a meal of several courses, further punctuated by minuscule amuse-bouches, moistened by a palpably good rosé, and enhanced by the evident joy and pride of the staff, whose pleasure in hosting definitely increased ours in eating— now seemed like a distant rosy memory of a kind of experience not likely to be repeated. I was no longer simply a traveler on vacation, strolling to meals or for a drink in the mild summer weather—enjoying the deep, restful, siesta-like quiet of a tiny French town, fostered by shuttered windows and broken only by the basilica's bells, or little blooms of chattering people emerging from behind closed doors. I was no longer a playful linguist, as I had been with our charming and charmable hôtelier, contending about which one of us got to "practice" the foreign language—in that manner of French conversation that always seems just a few millimeters short of outright flirting. His English was better than my French—which is well-pronounced, but still lacking in extensive vocabulary or great ease with verb tenses—so his ceding to my wish, at least some of the time, had felt like part of his affable hospitality. It was far too familiar, this feeling of my body defeating and disappointing me. I knew the drill.

Yet at this moment I wanted to say to our hôtelier, squatting near me again, juice in hand, as I sat on the sidewalk, "Alas, I'm afraid the wrist is broken," with a rueful smile that would lift me some millimeters out of being pathetic. But was *brisé* the right word for a fracture? Or the right word at all for "broken"? And what in heck was the word for "wrist"? I didn't think I'd ever had the occasion to use it. *Poignet*? Or was that some kind of knife? And what was I going to do about the fact that I really had to pee?

Before I could attempt to resolve these quandaries, the French Fire Department—the pompiers—arrived, I was helped onto a gurney inside their small truck by an attractive young woman whose boyfriend, I soon found out, was the driver, my husband secured our room in the hotel for another night, the siren was turned on and we were on the road to the nearest adequate hospital (in a town of about 50,000 some 20 kilometers away), my husband following in our rented car.

The young woman in the back of the fire truck with me was focused, concerned, personable. Her help felt small-scale, unofficious, perhaps not frequently enough given to become routine or boring for the givers. But to convey to her, across the language barrier, my urgent need, which, at this moment vied with the pain in my throbbing, meat-limp hand, seemed more uncomfortably personal than speaking English to an English-speaker, because my grip on connotation (having never said more than "*Pardonnez-moi, où sont les toilettes?*") was uncertain. Was the verb *pisser* which I settled on vulgar, or not? Should I have chanced *faire pipi* (or was that only for two-year-olds?), or even *uriner* (but wouldn't such formality make me sound bizarre?). The young woman offered a bedpan, and I tried to explain to her, with a number of left-handed gestures, that I was afraid I couldn't manage—lying down and one-handed, as I was. Hoping I sounded as polite as I meant to be, I asked for her promise to lead me to les toilettes as soon as we got to the hospital, and so we chatted about where I was from in California, and what I was doing in France, and where she'd gone when she visited Les États-Unis. Everyday non-substantive chit-chat not driven by necessity—even with a broken wrist and burning bladder, I wasn't half-bad at that.

~

An hour of dual discomfort later—including a transfer from the pompiers' gurney to the hospital's emergency room gurney, questioning, paperwork (not filled out by right-handed me)—and, finally, I was briefly allowed to stand and be led to the promised relief. The young woman departed quickly, I thanked her sincerely, waving my left hand, I was wheeled to an examination room, where, eventually, someone cleaned the wound and lightly bandaged it, and, after a while, a doctor entered and asked me the usual questions about my injury, and also, atypically, inquired about my work. He was relaxed and talkative—in the way that some doctors, cross-culturally, seem to train themselves to be, perhaps because of the high tension of their jobs; or, perhaps it was a bit interesting for him to talk to une étrangère in this regional hospital. I mentioned that I was a retired teacher of English literature and creative writing, that I had written a book on Shakespeare, and some books of poems, surprised that the French words for all of this were actually flowing, (finally under medical care, perhaps I relaxed a notch, and stopped second-guessing myself so much). The doctor picked up on the Shakespeare with evident interest and knowledge, remarking that the playwright was "un miracle!" coming almost out of no-where, and, as if we were having a conversation over glasses of wine at some intellectual soirée, I told him I understood exactly what he meant, that Marlowe, for example, born in the same year as Shakespeare, was nowhere near as complex or profound a playwright. On I went with my little French script of literary pleasantries, feeling the tang of pleasure as every third or fourth word that issued from my mouth surprised me that I knew it—in spite of my fears. Would I have to have my first surgery after a fracture and miss any or all of the few days my son, daughter-in-law and grandkids were going to be in Normandy? I was a woman over seventy, with a broken hand. A train wreck. But as I created my part in the continuing conversation I felt as if I were building an actual French edifice, placing my words like bricks, binding them with the mortar of my sentences. For these min-utes I was more than a woman "of a certain age" and a patient, more than a victim of chance, fragility, carelessness. I felt not the slightest quiver of disdain or distaste coming towards me. For all the French valorization of l'amour, la beauté, le plaisir (and the building-sized car ad featuring a naked young belle I had seen on a previous trip), this doctor did not make me feel the least bit typecast as an old woman. I felt *seen*. An American doctor, even an interesting and surprisingly literary one, surely would not have pleased me this much!

The Shakespeare-loving doctor also saw that my hand was

definitively fractured, though he ordered an X-ray, nevertheless. And soon, my husband—moral support and sounding board—having been allowed to join us, we were all talking, while I occasionally translated—almost as if I were participating in a planned conference involving French and English speakers—about my options for surgery. The doctor explained that we *could* go to Paris, but assured us with some chest-inflating pride that medicine in France was much more centralized than it was in the U.S., so there wouldn't be *that* much difference between my treatment in the capital and in this regional hospital. I couldn't imagine being in the car for several hours with an open wound, clutching my arm, then starting the process of being admitted all over again someplace much more crowded. A surgeon was going to be available and surgery could take place today, where we were. And if I'd had to chose a travel destination to fracture bones in, France, with a medical system often rated best in the world, would certainly have been it. I was down in the pit of the situation again now, on the ride, resigned, surrendered. But there was something beyond that: the glow of my love of the language, the country, the culture, was cast over this hospital and its workers, too, as if they could do no wrong. At this moment, it was as if I had a path laid out before me—the challenge of dredging up and gathering French words into my net, in order to propel myself through this cross-cultural experience with a modicum of aplomb—and negotiating that path would occupy most of my cerebral neurons, thus pushing most fears aside. Had I spoken French without mind-filling premeditation, or any sense of intrinsic glamour, I just might have felt, or even proceeded, differently.

~

Within an hour or so, I was in a room, reading a book I had with me, having given most of my personal possessions to my husband, who finally went back to our hotel, and in search of a meal. I'm quite sure I was given a pill for pain, but I'm not sure I asked what it was; uncharacteristically passive, I may have just accepted it from the tiny corrugated cup handed to me, although, in the very few hospitalizations for surgery I'd had in California, I'd inquired scrupulously about all medications. Perhaps my brain was spent with summoning and trying to understand the French I needed to navigate my situation; perhaps the glow of French was enough to turn it off.

Time passed slowly until a startlingly squat and coarse-face woman, contrasting noticeably with the lithe and quite lovely nurses, arrived to take me to the shower. She placed the carbolic soap I was to scrub with in my left hand, then finished the job brusquely and efficiently herself since my out-of-commission right hand made it incomplete. She washed my thick, curly hair with something prickly that left it sticking out in all directions. She didn't exude any charm; the few shreds I tried to send her way dissipated in the air. When I asked her if she happened to have any conditioner, she laughed. I wondered why I wasn't a little more weirded out. Was it my realism and resignation kicking in again at this particularly *un*glowing moment, or had there been something more than a painkiller in that pill? In any case, when you submit yourself for care, whether in your native language and land or in a foreign one, you have little choice but to get with the program.

In the busy area I was next taken to on a gurney, sometime later, someone I surmised was an anesthesiologist gave me a nerve block in my arm; I was reassured that my preference for a local anesthetic had apparently been heeded. He seemed pleasant, but, not surprisingly, my conversation with him was very limited. When he asked how I was doing, I blurted *J'ai peur* ("I'm afraid"), at least in part because I wasn't sufficiently sure of the word for "nervous." Then he asked me if I was on vacation and where I was going next, in what seemed a well-intentioned effort at diversion. Had I sufficient faith in my linguistic instincts and the incredible number of cognates to English words in French, I might have spoken in a less alarmist way, preserving my sang-froid, or at least its appearance: *Je suis* un peu *nerveuse*—"I'm *a little* nervous" (and even gotten the feminine ending of the adjective correct). But of course, the anesthesiologist's main concern was whether I felt *douleur,* "pain." I wasn't entirely sure (*was* that nerve block working?), but I said "I don't *think* I feel pain," giving the anesthesiologist the benefit of the doubt. At that precise moment, perhaps I didn't focus well enough on rounding my lips for the vowels of *douleur,* because in a little while I heard him laughing, saying something about "dollar" to someone else, mocking my American pronunciation. It was snide. Perhaps worse, did his speaking within range of me mean he didn't think I understood much French at all? Suddenly I felt the same way I might in crowded American hospitals, not *seen,* invisible, out of hearing, just another body on a gurney. I thought, as I often had in clinics and hospitals: medical procedures are routine for doctors, but unique for the patient. And then, a parallel thought: speaking a language is routine for the native speaker, but uniquely and riskily adventurous for the foreigner. And then I was routinely wheeled into the operating room, having my hand poked with something sharp, and being asked, again, if I felt pain. And then—expressed wish for only local anesthesia perhaps necessarily by the by—I was out.

~

I awoke peaceably in recovery—and remarkably without the slightest tinge of nausea (score that point for French medicine)—where the nurse asked me if I would like to speak to my husband, and, amazingly (score again), also handed me my cell phone on which to call; I had no recollection of arranging for the disposition of my phone. Eventually I was taken to my room, where my loyal husband, having made another trip to the hospital, found me fantasizing, mouth watering (having had nothing but orange juice all day), about those never bought or eaten pastries so flaky and sweet. After he left for the night, the nurse on duty seemed to be getting me ready for bedtime; she looked somewhat surprised when I mentioned food. I couldn't even remember, in that moment, the simple addition of *très* ("very"), that would increase the intensity of *J'ai faim* ("I'm hungry"). But at last, about 10 P.M., a bowl of some modestly tasty thick creamed soup arrived and I devoured it.

It was difficult to find a comfortable position in which to sleep, my hand—seemingly only fragilely bandaged and protected—hurt, it was very hot in the un-air-conditioned room, and my roommate on the other side of my and her protective bed curtains, who sounded older than me and crazy, continually moaned and talked loudly to herself. The rose-tinted glasses through which I tended to see the French were losing more of their hue: it was clear that the nurses were no more capable of handling this patient than nurses anywhere else might be, and favored the cognizant and in control; they scolded her, and told her to behave. But one of them very kindly brought me a portable fan, and I slept, on and off.

I didn't know my exact diagnosis, or even whether someone had communicated it to me, and I had failed to understand; I certainly didn't know how my surgery had gone. But I was focused on getting released in the morning, which I heartily hoped to do, since we were already missing a day with my son and his family and would not see them after this planned visit for a very long time! For that reason, I told every nurse who came into the room while I was awake that I wanted to see the surgeon as soon as possible; they seemed very deferential at the mention of his name, perhaps protecting his time as nurses everywhere might do. At some point in the morning, he was announced, and I looked up to see him at the foot of my bed, speaking quite quickly, and saying something I wasn't fully getting, although I think I was emotionally and linguistically prepared only for non-substantive pleasantries, for being released back to being a tourist en vacances—although one armed with pain pills and antibiotics, and fully prepared to check her progress with doctors once back home. The surgeon said something about the bones in my hand being very soft—not very surprising, given my osteoporosis. I waited to hear the qualification, as in *But everything went very well and we expect you to make a full recovery.* Instead I heard a slightly unexpected emphasis on *hope*, and on his *best efforts*, even something about the available *equipment* for the surgery, which dinged in my brain, but didn't develop enough speed to burst through the barrier of my desire to see my family, and— as now seemed possible, if somewhat tricky—to resume the pleasures of travel so delightfully bracketed from ordinary life. After all, I was on vacation, I was in France, and I was, *un miracle!* speaking, if not always completely understanding, French. And then the surgeon exited the room.

~

The procedures of release, involving some technical or uncommon words I had little grasp of, upped the opaqueness quotient; I felt little more attuned to the situation than my husband, at my side again, having made yet another trip from our hotel. I certainly did not recognize the word for the rigid Velcro-closing brace that was needed to protect my wrist and hand, and it wasn't clear whether it would be provided at the hospital (it eventually was), or have to be procured outside. Furthermore, apparently, as I finally grasped, I would be required to have the dressing on my wound changed and the wound cleaned every two days during our remaining days in France by a licensed nurse whom we would have to locate in whatever town we were in or near. And we would have to purchase a very generous collection of supplies from a drugstore, to bring to these nurses—a large variety of bandages and a number of antiseptics. (Painkillers and an antibiotic were provided at the hospital.) Free at last, we paid the hospital bill, which was remarkably modest, and certainly renewed our appreciation for the single-payer French medical system (the pompiers had cost nothing at all!) and drove back to our little town, where I felt compelled to wash my hideous hair in the sink in our hotel room with my left hand and a little coerced help from my husband, and where, afterwards, we procured that cornucopia of bandages and antiseptics (costing almost a fifth of the amount for the surgery and hospitalization) at the local drugstore. Then, finalement! we were off, with one stop on the auto-route to have a snack and buy a couple of cheap comfy pillows to rest my hand on as my husband drove. Now, clearly, there was no thought of cutting short our plans to go to Normandy and to spend a little time in the Loire Valley, afterwards, before flying home from Paris. Yes, there was pain, and some worry. And it wasn't easy, as it turned out, for foreigners—one of whom was awkwardly one-handed and whose other hand was aching—to figure out how to search for the appropriate kind of nurses, to find their names and numbers, then phone them, and locate them, every other day. But it was all part of an anthropology of travel, of experiencing a slightly different medical system from the inside, almost as a native would. How curious it was that each nurse had a different method for cleaning, dressing and bandaging. How amusing that one of them suggested that we didn't need half the supplies we had purchased that we were lugging around (and we donated them on the spot). How fortunate, after all, that it was "only" my hand this time, and not a knee or a leg. A hand is kind of remote from the rest of the body, isn't it? From the torso, especially—with all its vital organs, a center of "the self." And one has an extra. If slowly, and with great care, I could at least walk up and down the staircase in the beautiful stone farmhouse in Normandy where we joined our children and grandkids (so amazing and marvelous to see right in front of us!). And, after that, with even greater care, I could walk up the banister-less soft stone steps of the circular staircase to our room in a hotel on a narrow medieval street in Chinon in the Loire, holding on to the wall and the occasional rope "railing." The hôtelier there, eyeing my bandaged hand in its rigid brace, told my husband he could park in his private garage, rather than the one normally used by guests, from which there was quite a climb. And, as on previous visits, my conversational, non-technical French seemed to have improved with exposure to the language around me; my brain was even less occupied with premeditation as I spoke. À la fin, on line for hours at Charles de Gaulle for our very delayed flight back to California, I became engaged in conversation with a young Frenchman, who barely seemed to notice the brace on my hand, and told me my French surprised him, because it didn't have an American accent at all! Once again, my glasses took on that lovely rose tint. I felt so un-pigeonholed, so happily *seen*, and the glow lasted, though my wrist hurt, the hours-late plane was crowded and cramped, and there was no hot food on the flight because of a fire at the suppliers.

If one is going to break a bone that requires surgery (but conveniently doesn't impede walking), there's something to be said for doing so on holiday in a foreign culture one loves, whose language is a source of delight, and palpable—in the mouth, on the tongue, in the nose, in the busy mind—and not well enough spoken not to be—every sentence emerging with a mental pat on one's own back. How lovely to remain traveling, on vacation, released from duty and routine, seeing a little bit of the inside of another culture, every sight new; how lovely to feel one has the power to summon up that language one admires, and to maintain one's pride by not mangling it utterly beyond recognition. Such delights and desires ultimately burnished a difficult if not impossible situation, distracted me, pulled me through.

~

Just two weeks later, I am following up at the first available appointment in a clinic near my home in Southern California, having my hand fluoroscoped by a remarkably bouncy young hand surgeon. I am not on vacation, not shaping words in a foreign tongue that please and distract me; I am only a patient. And he is saying, "Hmm, that looks pretty good, yeah," and I am thinking *adventure over* until he looks at another view and says "Uh-oh, there are some issues here." He ponders for a while, then tells me—as the French general surgeon's words about soft bone, and *hope* and *best efforts* and even *equipment* revive in my mind—that there is an area of very gravelly bone, and that the metal plate and pin I have in my wrist now

The author, with wrist brace, still traveling in France, after surgery in Brittany. July, 2017.

APARTNESS

are not adequate supports; the plate is too small. (Much later, when I actually read the surgery report, I see that "the distal radius was extremely *comminuted*," which I have to look up: apparently it describes a fracture producing multiple bone splinters.) The energetic and quite kindly hand surgeon says he understands that undergoing revision surgery so soon is not an appealing idea, but if I want to recover full use of my right hand, he thinks it's necessary. And that turns out to be true: after quite a few months of fairly arduous therapy, I do make a fine recovery. And, he goes on, "the French just aren't up to American standards in equipment, by the way." I am certainly far from thrilled to be operated on again, but I feel no anger towards the French general surgeon or anyone on his hospital's medical staff. I had no real choice, and they really did do their best. A relatively small regional hospital—probably not as well equipped as a Parisian one, after all—they just didn't have the right plate.

So, the next day, I am once again lying on a gurney, waiting hours for surgery, an old hand (ha!) at the drill, and having to pee. But it's easier to ask about that in English, and soon I'm wheeling my IV pole to the restroom. The nurses, and the anesthesiologist who comes by later, are all very cheerful and willing to answer questions. But, compared to some of the French emergency and medical personnel, especially to the Shakespeare-loving admitting doctor, they seem more bound by their roles, and more likely to require me to play mine as patient; their veneers stay on. I'm the only one left in the pre-operative holding area. I rebel a little. I sing, "It's my surgery, and I'll cry if I want to, cry if I want to." At least one person at the nurse's station chuckles.

~

Pushing three years later, I am even more careful than I was, no matter how enticed. I am grateful for my functioning right hand. I am grateful to have, thus far, broken no more bones. A nanosecond of slip, so delicate a rupture, has so extended a consequence, and powerfully reasserts the brittleness of the armature supporting our bodies. But what a miracle to heal from physical wounds, and even more importantly, from a destructive sense of our own fragility, to manage to live in the present as much as we do, to move with anticipation towards the next moments of plaisir and joie—the past not prologue, but ancient history—until that day, hopefully in the far and hardly imaginable future, when we no longer can.

The author, wrist cast just removed, months after revision surgery in California. 2017.

4 A.M., Suddenly Awake

And I'm on a tiny island
in a frigid, obsidian
sea, and the beloved sleeper,
Hoar-Beard, beside me,
remote as his own ghost,
as if he's already sailed
to the unimaginable continent,
as one day he must—
unless I sail first.
Silence pings in my ears. I can taste
the ultimate aloneness like metal
on my tongue. I imagine grasping
a routine: put on slippers,
pull up sheets, fluff
the desolate pillows,
smooth the coverlet—like a kid holding on
to a blanket edge between knuckle
and thumb, milking it.
But next I hear the whistle
as the milk starts to steam and froth
for espresso, and it's morning, morning!
commonplace and miraculous
as the sleeper, awake
and hale, breezy in the kitchen
where we meet, as eggs for two popped
into the skillet like summer suns breaking free
of the sea's hold, bursting
into the sky, sizzling—
And the night an aberration
and a lie.

Endnotes

1. Susan Koppelman, "*Belles Lettres* Interview" with Merrill Joan Gerber, *Belles Lettres* 5, No. 3 (Spring 1990), 16.

2. *Kansas Quarterly* 24, Nos. 2 & 3 (1992), 116.

3. Transcript of interview conducted May 19, 2011, with Nell Cochrane Taylor, by Sarah Dunn. Smith College Alumnae Oral History Project, https://media.smith.edu/departments/archives/alumoh/transcripts/TaylorN.pdf , 8.

4. Colin Campbell, "The Tyranny of the Yale Critics," *The New York Times Magazine* (February 9, 1986). http://www.nytimes.com/1986/02/09/magazine/the-tyranny-of-the-yale-critics.html?pagewanted=all, 2.

5. Larissa MacFarquahar, "The Prophet of Decline: Harold Bloom's Influential Anxieties," *The New Yorker* (September 30, 2002), 89.

6. Campbell, "The Tyranny of the Yale Critics," 2.

7. Philip Roth, *Exit Ghost* (New York: Houghton Mifflin Company, 2007), 244. The passage conti"Breaking Pattern" on page 194nues: "George [Plimpton] afforded my first glimpse of privilege and its vast rewards—he seemingly had nothing to escape, no flaw to hide or injustice to defy or defect to compensate for or weakness to overcome or obstacle to circumvent, appearing instead to have learned everything and to be open to everything altogether effortlessly. I'd never imagined getting anywhere without the unstinting persistence in which my hardworking family had diligently schooled me; George would have known from the outset all he was automatically destined for."

8. Jane Hirshfield, "The Question of Originality," *The American Poetry Review* 18, No. 4 (July/August 1989), 8.

9. William Stafford, *Writing the Australian Crawl: Views on the Writer's Vocation* (Ann Arbor, Michigan: University of Michigan Press, 1978), 3.

10. *The Norton Anthology of English Literature*, 5th edition, Vol. 1, M.H. Abrams, General Editor (New York, New York: W.W. Norton & Company, 1986), p. 1210.

11. Neither my children nor I knew then what we have since learned—that my father's niece Charlotte was sent on a Kindertransport to Amsterdam late in 1938, but perished, nevertheless, in Auschwitz, in 1944.

12. John Donne, Holy Sonnet IX, *The Complete Poetry and Selected Prose of John Donne*, edited by Charles M. Coffin (New York: Random House, 1952), p. 250

13. *The English Poems of George Herbert*, edited by C.A. Patrides (London: Dent & Sons, Ltd., 1974), p. 67.

14. Originally published in *Cyclamens and Swords*, April, 2012. Reprinted in *Bird Flying through the Banquet* (Lexington, Kentucky: FutureCycle Press, 2017).

15. "Terrific Mother," in Lorrie Moore, *Birds of America* (New York: Alfred A. Knopf, 1998), p. 268

16. *Mishkan T'Filah: A Reform Siddur* (New York: CCAR Press, 2007).

17. *The Norton Anthology of Modern Poetry*, 2nd edition, edited by Richard Ellmann and Robert O'Clair, p. 1059.

18. *The English Poems of George Herbert*, p. 172.

About the Author

Judy Kronenfeld's six full-length books of poetry include *If Only There Were Stations of the Air* (Sheila-Na-Gig Editions, 2024), *Groaning and Singing* (FutureCycle, 2022), *Bird Flying through the Banquet* (FutureCycle, 2017), *Shimmer* (WordTech, 2012), and *Light Lowering in Diminished Sevenths*, 2nd edition (Antrim House, 2012)—winner of the 2007 Litchfield Review Poetry Book Prize. Her third chapbook is *Oh Memory, You Unlocked Cabinet of Amazements!* (Bamboo Dart Press, 2024). Her poems have appeared in such journals as *Cimarron Review*, *DMQ Review*, *Gyroscope Review*, *MacQueen's Quinterly*, *New Ohio Review*, *Offcourse*, *One (Jacar Press)*, *One Art*, *Rattle*, *Sheila-Na-Gig*, *Valparaiso Poetry Review*, and *Verdad*.

ABOUT INLANDIA INSTITUTE

The Inlandia Institute is a regional literary non-profit and publishing house. We seek to bring focus to the richness of the literary enterprise that has existed in this region for ages.

The mission of Inlandia Books is to recognize, support, and expand literary activity in Inland Southern California by publishing works which deepen people's awareness, understanding, and appreciation of this unique, complex and creatively vibrant region. The mission is carried out by actively seeking out new works by writers who are affiliated with the region, and also through national literary competitions which elevate Inlandia Books to the national literary stage.

To learn more about the Inlandia Institute, please visit our website at www.InlandiaInstitute.org.

SELECTED INLANDIA BOOKS

Writing from Inlandia annual anthology series
Guajira, the Cuba girl by Zita Arocha
Breaking Pattern by Tisha Marie Reichle-Aguilera
Exit Prohibited by Ellen Estilai
These Black Bodies Are..., edited by Romaine Washington
Vermillion Speedateer by Sebraé Harris
Pretend Plumber by Stephanie Barbé Hammer
Ladybug by Nikia Chaney
Vital: The Future of Healthcare, edited by RM Ambrose
Güero-Güero: The White Mexican and Other Published and Unpublished Stories by Dr. Eliud Martínez
A Short Guide to Finding Your First Home in the United States: An Inlandia anthology on the immigrant experience
Care: Stories by Christopher Records
San Bernardino, Singing, edited by Nikia Chaney
Facing Fire: Art, Wildfire, and the End of Nature in the New West by Douglas McCulloh
In the Sunshine of Neglect: Defining Photographs and Radical Experiments in Inland Southern California,1950 to the Present by Douglas McCulloh
More Dreamers of the Golden Dream by Susan Straight and Delphine Sims with photographs by Douglas McCulloh
Orangelandia: The Literature of Inland Citrus edited by Gayle Brandeis
While We're Here We Should Sing by The Why Nots
Go to the Living by Micah Chatterton
No Easy Way: Integrating Riverside Schools - A Victory for Community by Arthur L. Littleworth

www.ingramcontent.com/pod-product-compliance
Lightning Source LLC
Chambersburg PA
CBHW061523050726
47503CB00015B/2626